The Most Interesting People Who Live Life, Volume 2: 250 Anecdotes

David Bruce

Published by David Bruce, 2024.

THE MOST INTERESTING PEOPLE WHO LIVE LIFE, VOLUME 2: 250 ANECDOTES

First edition. January 15, 2024.

ISBN: 979-8224538539

Written by David Bruce.

Table of Contents

Dedication

Dedicated to Carl Eugene Bruce and Josephine Saturday Bruce

My father, Carl Eugene Bruce, died on 24 October 2013. He used to work for Ohio Power, and at one time, his job was to shut off the electricity of people who had not paid their bills. He sometimes would find a home with an impoverished mother and some children. Instead of shutting off their electricity, he would tell the mother that she needed to pay her bill or soon her electricity would be shut off. He would write on a form that no one was home when he stopped by because if no one was home he did not have to shut off their electricity.

The best good deed that anyone ever did for my father occurred after a storm that knocked down many power lines. He and other linemen worked long hours and got wet and cold. Their feet were freezing because water got into their boots and soaked their socks. Fortunately, a kind woman gave my father and the other linemen dry socks to wear.

My mother, Josephine Saturday Bruce, died on 14 June 2003. She used to work at a store that sold clothing. One day, an impoverished mother with a baby clothed in rags walked into the store and started shoplifting in an interesting way: The mother took the rags off her baby and dressed the infant in new clothing. My mother knew that this mother could not afford to buy the clothing, but she helped the mother dress her baby and then she watched as the mother walked out of the store without paying.

***

The doing of good deeds is important. As a free person, you can choose to live your life as a good person or as a bad person. To be a good person, do good deeds. To be a bad person, do bad deeds. If you do good deeds, you will become good. If you do bad deeds, you will become bad. To become the person you want to be, act as if you already are that kind of person. Each of us chooses what kind of person we will become. To become a good person, do the things a good person does. To become a bad person, do the things a bad person does. The opportunity to take action to become the kind of person you want to be is yours.

Human beings have free will. According to the Babylonian Niddah 16b, whenever a baby is to be conceived, the Lailah (angel in charge of contraception) takes the drop of semen that will result in the conception and asks God, "Sovereign of the Universe, what is going to be the fate of this drop? Will it develop into a robust or into a weak person? An intelligent or a stupid person? A wealthy or a poor person?" The Lailah asks all these questions, but it does not ask, "Will it develop into a righteous or a wicked person?" The answer to that question lies in the decisions to be freely made by the human being that is the result of the conception.

A Buddhist monk visiting a class wrote this on the chalkboard: "EVERYONE WANTS TO SAVE THE WORLD, BUT NO ONE WANTS TO HELP MOM DO THE DISHES." The students laughed, but the monk then said, "Statistically, it's highly unlikely that any of you will ever have the opportunity to run into a burning orphanage and rescue an infant. But, in the smallest gesture of kindness — a warm smile, holding the door for the person behind you, shoveling the driveway of the elderly person next door — you have committed an act of immeasurable profundity, because to each of us, our life is our universe."

Cover Photograph for *The Most Interesting People Who Live Life, Volume 2: 250 Anecdotes*:

Victoria Borodonova

https://pixabay.com/photos/woman-costume-clown-model-5780949/

https://www.instagram.com/victoriaborodinova/

https://www.facebook.com/victoria.borodinova

https://pixabay.com/users/victoria_borodinova-6314823/

****

Anecdotes are usually short humorous stories. Sometimes they are thought-provoking or informative, not amusing.

Do you know a language other than English? If you do, I give you permission to translate this book, copyright your translation, publish or self-publish it, and keep all the royalties for yourself.

Chapter 1: From Actors and Entertainers to Coaches

Actors and Entertainers

• Actors join acting companies for different reasons. Robert Stephens joined England's National Theatre simply because John Dexter asked him to play the Dauphin in *St. Joan* — a part for which he thought he was unsuited physically. Mr. Stephens told Mr. Dexter, "I'll join immediately, because I don't think anybody would ever offer me that part."[1]

• Liliane Montovecchi was a stage star of the Follies-Bergère, an occupation in which she made members of the audience happy. Tommy Tune met her later and asked her, "Don't you remember sitting in my lap at the Follies-Bergère?" She replied, "How could I remember? I sat on everybody's lap!"[2]

• Actor Douglas Fairbanks became infatuated with European royalty. Charlie Chaplin, who grew up poor, once brought him back down to Earth by asking, "Hullo, Douglas, how's the duke?" "What duke?" "Oh, any duke."[3]

Alcohol

• The Doubner Maggid once ate dinner at the house of a wealthy man, who urged him to drink. The Maggid drank one glass of wine, and the wealthy man asked him to drink another, which the Maggid did, despite protesting, "I am not accustomed to drinking." When the second glass of wine was empty, the wealthy man urged the Maggid to drink a third glass, so the Maggid asked him to fill the glass to the brim. When the glass was full, the Maggid told the man to pour more, surprising him, because — as he pointed out — the glass was already full. "There is a lesson in this," the Maggid said. "The glass is a lifeless object and it holds only a certain amount. This is even more true of a human being, who has life and will power and therefore should know the limit of his capacity for alcohol."[4]

• A judge got very drunk and then took off his robe and lay under a tree half-naked to sleep. Mulla Nasrudin came along, saw the judge, and took his cloak. Later, the judge sobered up, returned to his village and saw Nasrudin wearing his cloak. "Is that your cloak?" the judge asked. "No, it is not," Nasrudin replied. "I saw a very drunk man lying under a tree, asleep, and I took his cloak so that robbers would not steal it. I should like very much to find that man so that I can return his cloak." Fearing lest his friends and neighbors find out that it was he who had been drunk, the judge replied, "Such a drunken fellow deserves what happens to him," and then he left Nasrudin and the cloak alone.[5]

• The Hassidim abhorred drunkenness, but they felt that a drink after prayers was appropriate. Once, Rabbi Israel of Rizhyn was asked why the Hassidim took a drink after prayers while the opponents of Hassidism (the Mitnagdim) studied the Mishna instead of taking a drink. He answered, "The Mitnagdim pray frigidly, without life, enthusiasm, or emotion. They appear almost lifeless. After their prayers, they study the Mishna — an appropriate subject when one mourns the dead. But the prayers of the Hassidim are alive and living people need a drink."[6]

• When Casey Driessen was in junior high school, his parents bribed him. They told him that if he stayed away from illegal drugs and tobacco and alcohol until he was 21 years old that they would give him $1,000. He accepted the challenge, and he didn't cheat. When people would ask why he didn't cheat, he would say, "Could you take $1,000 from your parents?" When he turned 21 years old — at midnight when December 5 changed to December 6 — he took his very first sip of beer.[7]

• Some pro athletes make sure to be good role models for the kids who idolize them. Major-league pitcher Nolan Ryan gave up chewing tobacco when he saw some Little Leaguers chewing it. And when NBA star Bobby Jones accepted an award from a liquor company after a computer analysis stated that he was the most effective NBA player, Mr. Jones thanked the liquor company but also stated that he did not drink alcohol.[8]

• Russian bass Fyodor Chaliapin enjoyed partying all night even though he knew that it would interfere with his singing the following day. American industrialist Henry Ford once offered him a large sum of money to sing at 10:30 a.m., but Mr. Chaliapin replied, "Unfortunately, at that early hour I cannot even spit."[9]

• A preacher once spoke in his sermon about the dangers of alcohol. At one point, he asked an elderly lady — one of the pillars of the church — if she agreed that alcohol was an evil that should be destroyed. The elderly woman replied, "Actually, I enjoy a little toddy once in a while."[10]

Animals

• At one time, zoos kept large animals such as gorillas in small cages. Now, zoos prefer to have larger, more open spaces that resemble the animals' habitat as much as possible and in which the animals can roam around. The open spaces make the viewing experience more pleasurable for the zoos' visitors, and the open spaces make the animals happier and more likely to breed in captivity. The first person to design larger, more open spaces for the display and comfort of animals was Karl Hagenbeck, who in 1907 placed antelopes and lions near each other in the Hamburg Zoo in Germany — the lions were kept away from the antelopes by an impassible moat. Today, zoos will keep prey animals further away from predator animals. To make the zoo settings resemble the animals' natural habitat, zoo workers will do such things as force animals in a tropical forest setting to take shelter a few times a day when zoo workers create artificial rain showers. During the showers, the zoo workers flash strobe lights for lightning and play recordings of thunder and the shrieks of howler monkeys and the calls of birds. All of these things make the animals feel more at home.[11]

• The 1,049-mile-long Iditarod Trail Sled Dog Race in Alaska is taken seriously. During and after the race the urine of the sled dogs used in the race is tested to make sure the dogs have not been given any performance-enhancing drugs. Preparation for the race is also time-consuming — and not just the training. For each race, Susan Butcher, who won the Iditarod four times, and her friends made up a thousand dog booties to protect the sled dogs' feet from such hazards as sharp rocks and sharp shards of ice. In addition, she made up about 75 burlap bags of dog food — while racing, her dogs will each eat about 8,000 calories daily. For each Iditarod, she needed about 1,500 pounds of supplies, much of it left at the various race checkpoints.[12]

• When war correspondent and photographer Margaret Bourke-White received permission to fly on a bombing expedition during World War II, J. Hampton Atkinson piloted her himself, saying, "I'm going to fly you myself because if you die, I want to die, too." (Fortunately, neither of them died.) By the way, while photographer Ms. Bourke-White was attending the University of Michigan in the early 1920s, she kept something strange in her dormitory room bathtub — a pet milk snake.[13]

April Fool's Day

• On April Fool's Day, a small boy played a joke on a new schoolmaster, but the schoolmaster told him as punishment to write out in full the sixth declension in Latin ten times. All of the students were angry with the new schoolmaster for punishing a student for playing an April Fool's joke, but one small boy suddenly remembered that Latin has no sixth declension. After finding out that the joke was on them, the schoolboys liked the new schoolmaster.[14]

Art

• While famed photographer Yousuf Karsh was taking the portrait of artist Jean-Paul Riopelle, he admired a circular painting that the artist had completed. Mr. Karsh believed that the painting resembled a stained-glass rosette — an image that brings to mind stained-glass windows in cathedrals. Mr. Riopelle explained that he had a particular purpose in creating a painting with that particular shape: "I'll tell you why I did that. Because my dealers insist on setting the price of a canvas by the number of square inches in it. For the fun of it, I decided to confuse them and paint one that is round."[15]

• In New York, artist Louise Bourgeois held a salon on Sundays. One day, an artist called on the telephone and asked for permission to come to the salon. Ms. Bourgeois replied, "Who are you? What kind of work do you do? A painter? What size? ... All right. You could come at three o'clock. Don't come if you have a cold."[16]

Audiences

• Giuseppe de Stefano sang the high-B note at the end of *Celeste Aida* exactly the way that Verdi wanted it — softly — instead of the way his Catania, Sicily, audience wanted it — loudly. When the audience whistled in derision, Mr. de Stefano told them, "That's the way Verdi wrote it!" A know-it-all shouted back, "Verdi made a mistake!"[17]

• Dr. Samuel Johnson once played host to actress Mrs. Siddons, who often sold out theaters. The good doctor's servant proved to be very slow about getting a chair for her, so Dr. Johnson gave her this compliment: "You see, madam, wherever you go, there are no seats to be had."[18]

Automobiles

• Joe S, a regular reader of Bartcop Entertainment on the Web, remembers Saab automobiles from the 1960s. A friend of his ran into trouble with his Saab motor, so he disconnected it from the rest of the car, bolted a handle to it, and hitchhiked to Denver while carrying the motor by the handle to have it repaired. Joe S says, "I don't think Saabs are like that anymore."[19]

• Being a world-class gymnast has both advantages and disadvantages. An advantage for Russian gymnast Svetlana Khorkina was that it allowed her to buy a car. A disadvantage is that she found it difficult to find the spare time to learn how to drive it.[20]

Baseball and Softball

• In the 1953 World Series, Dodger pitcher Carl Erskine loaded the bases in the first inning, and Yankee Billy Martin hit a triple. Mr. Erskine was taken out of the game. This made him determined to do better in his next game. In game three of the World Series, he won, 3-2, and after the game another Dodger pitcher, Preacher Roe, told him, "Great game! Do you know you set a World Series strikeout record?" Without realizing it, because of his determination to make up for his previous failure in game one, Mr. Erskine had struck out 14 batters in a World Series game — a record that stood for 10 years.[21]

• When major-league pitcher Christy Mathewson was a kid, he used to play a game he called "hailey over," in which he would throw a baseball over the roof of a barn to another kid. Once, he threw the baseball too strongly and broke a neighbor's window. When he was a boy as well as when he was a man, he had good character, so he paid the neighbor the money it cost to fix the window. His mother said, "It took Christy a long time to save the dollar the broken window cost, but it taught him a sense of responsibility."[22]

• Dodger catcher Roy Campanella used to tell Dodger pitchers, "Now you young pitchers just throw what ol' Roy calls and I'll make you a winner." After losing a game, however, Dodger pitcher Carl Erskine would show Mr. Campanella the box score that said, "Erskine losing pitcher," and ask him whether instead it should say, "Campanella losing catcher." Mr. Campanella would laugh and reply, "You can always shake me off."[23]

• Two nuns went to a baseball game, but a couple of guys sitting behind them began complaining about Catholics. One guy said, "We ought to go to a place where there are only 100 Catholics." The other guy said, "Better still, let's go to a place where there are only 50

Catholics." One of the nuns turned around and said, "Why don't you go to Hell, where you won't find any Catholics."[24]

• Softball great Joan Joyce pitched over 100 no-hit games. Baseball great Ted Williams had a season batting average of .406 in 1941 and ended his career with a lifetime batting average of .344. The two met in 1963 in a ballpark at Waterbury, Connecticut. In ten minutes, Ms. Joyce pitched 40 pitches to Mr. Williams. With those 40 chances, Mr. Williams managed to get one hit.[25]

• Jimmy Piersall was an amazing center fielder who could both make seemingly impossible catches and rifle the baseball to home plate. Manager Casey Stengel was once asked if his team would run on Mr. Piersall. Mr. Stengel replied, "Oh, sure. We'll run on him — every time somebody hits the ball over the center-field fence."[26]

Books

• Librarian Malcolm Glenn Wyer decided to accept a position with the Denver Public Library after having worked for years in university libraries. One of his friends wondered why he would want to work in a public library, which was engaged in the distribution of "trivial worthless current fiction." Mr. Wyer replied that he thought it would be interesting to move from a university library, where 90% of the circulation was by students who were working to complete mandatory assignments, to a public library, where 90% of the circulation was by citizens who were interested in reading for its own sake.[27]

• TV's Mister Rogers went into television because so much TV was bad, and he knew it could be better. Of course, much TV remains bad, and when he wasn't working, Mister Rogers watched little TV. He once told a friend that he didn't want to sound elitist, but he simply preferred reading a book to watching television.[28]

• A ghostwriter once asked female jockey Robyn Smith for permission to write her autobiography for her, but she asked why he instead didn't ghost the autobiography of fellow jockey Donna

Hillman. He said, "Donna Hillman? The pretty one?" Ms. Smith replied, "No, I'm the pretty one."[29]

• When businessman and statesman Bernard Baruch was asked what book he would most want to have with him if he were shipwrecked on a desert island, he replied, "A practical guide to boat building."[30]

Children

• In his book *Kids Say the Darnest Things!* Art Linkletter writes about a time when he asked viewers of his *House Party* TV program to send in funny things their children had written. One boy had written a letter to the President of the United States: "Dere Mister President. I would like you to send children [to] Mars in the next space ship going in that direction. I would appreciate it very much. One of your future voters: Mitchell." Mr. Linkletter writes that this note was attached to young Mitchell's letter: "Dear Mr. President: As the parents of Mitchell Miller, we would like to give you our permission to send Mitchell anywhere into space."[31]

• Pope John XXIII once visited the Benedictine Abbey of Subiaco, which is located south of Rome. Crowds of people arrived to see the Pope, and several boys with dirty shoes climbed up on a valuable carved antique choir stall so that they could see the Pope better. Some sacristans started to chase the boys away, but Pope John XXIII stopped them, saying, "Leave them alone; let them stay there. Their conscience is still quite pure."[32]

• Bonnie Hellum Brechill's five-year-old daughter started playing with a little Amish girl, although the Amish girl spoke a Pennsylvania Dutch dialect. Later, Ms. Brechill asked her daughter if she had understood anything the Amish girl had spoken — she had not. Ms. Brechill then asked, "But you played so nicely together. How?" Her daughter replied, "We understood each other's giggles."[33]

• Even as a youngster, Jennifer Lopez was feisty. During a fight with her sister, she once held a knife in her hand and chased her.

When she was in the fourth grade, she learned that a person whom she thought was a friend had been spreading rumors about her. She stood up for herself, demanded respect, fought the "friend," and knocked her down.[34]

• When Nasrudin was a small boy, he was bothered by a young bully who claimed that no one could trick him. One day, Nasrudin went to the bully and told him, "If you wait here, I will trick you like you have never been tricked before." Then Nasrudin went away, leaving the bully to wait for him until the bully realized that Nasrudin was not going to return.[35]

• Some audience members talk way too much during viewings at movie theaters. During the showing of the *Star Trek: The Next Generation* movie, *First Contact*, a man kept talking, so a 10-year-old *Star Trek* fan turned around in her seat and asked him, "Jerk, can you *spell* 'Prime Directive'?"[36]

• Nancy Lopez learned how to play golf from her auto mechanic father, Domingo. Even when she was a child, her parents taught her that she was special. Once she started washing the dishes, but her father stopped her, saying, "Those hands are meant for golf, not dishes."[37]

• As a young girl of 16, Emma Abbott was so eager to hear opera singer Parepa-Rosa in New York that she played her guitar and sang to earn money while traveling from Illinois to New York — and did not hear Parepa-Rosa, because the prima donna was ill.[38]

• Abraham Lincoln grew a beard after reading a letter from 11-year-old Grace Bedell of New York, who thought the beard would make his thin face "look a great deal better." She also wrote, "All the ladies like whiskers."[39]

• Occasionally, children will attempt to recite Biblical passages, but not realize that their memory is faulty. One small boy recited the Ninth Commandment as "Thou shalt not covet thy neighbor's wife in vain."[40]

• In 1968, Russian tanks rumbled into Czechoslovakia to help with "troublemakers." One of the Czech children throwing pebbles at the Russian tanks was future Wimbledon champion Martina Navratilova.[41]

• As a little girl, jockey Julie Krone was a tomboy. Once, she was climbing a tree when her father saw her and warned, "Better look out. You'll fall!" Young Julie calmly replied, "I already did. Watch me climb."[42]

• As children, sisters Karen and Michelle Kwan used to wake up at 4:30 a.m. so they could be driven to an ice rink and practice ice skating. To save time in the morning, they used to sleep in their skating clothes.[43]

Christmas

• Political cartoonist Thomas Nast put his artistic skills to use during the Christmas season. In addition to creating drawings of Santa Claus for the newspapers and magazines he worked for, Mr. Nast also decorated his house for Christmas morning. When his children woke up, they discovered lots of giant paper dolls decorating the room where the gifts were found.[44]

• Elite American gymnast Shannon Miller got into gymnastics through accident. Her parents bought her a trampoline as a Christmas present when she was four years old, but after seeing her jump with abandon on it, they were afraid that she would hurt herself, so they enrolled her in gymnastics classes instead.[45]

• Before Christmas, a Sunday school teacher asked her students what kind of presents the infant Jesus would like and use. One student replied the baby Jesus would like disposable diapers because "Jesus was a real baby. Real babies need diapers."[46]

Clothing

• Mulla Nasrudin was invited to a feast, but because he was wearing ragged clothing, the servers ignored him and served the finely dressed guests instead. So Nasrudin returned home, changed into his best clothing, and then returned to the feast, where he was immediately served. At the feast, Nasrudin deliberately spilled soup on himself because he reasoned that the servers respected his clothing, not himself, and therefore his clothing ought to have a share of the feast.[47]

• Players in the All American Girls Professional Baseball League during the 1940s and 1950s were required to wear feminine attire while appearing in public. For example, a player might wear pants while traveling on the team bus, but if she got off the bus to go to the bathroom, she had to put on a skirt.[48]

Coaches

• When Gabrielle Reece started playing volleyball at Florida State University, her coach, Cecile Reynaud, knew that she needed to make a lot of improvement, and so Coach Reynaud had Ms. Reece practice serving the ball to the middle. To motivate Ms. Reece to do her best, Coach Reynaud would order the entire team to run a suicide drill whenever a ball did not hit the desired spot on the court. Coach Reynaud was a good life coach as well as a good volleyball coach. When Ms. Reece had a chance to model as well as play volleyball, Coach Reynaud advised her to do both, but to remember to concentrate on whatever she was supposed to concentrate on at a particular time. In Coach Reynaud's words, "When you are here, you're here. When you are there, you are there."[49]

• Whittier College football coach George Allen had a strict rule against his players smoking, so if a player with a cigarette in his mouth saw him coming, the player would quickly throw the cigarette to the ground and hope that Mr. Allen would not see it. One day, however, Mr. Allen did see the lit cigarette, and he asked the player, "What about that cigarette?" The player replied, "You can have it — you saw it first."[50]

Chapter 2: From Crime to Fathers

Crime

• A monk stole a valuable book from Abbot Anastasius and took it to a book dealer to sell. The dealer looked at the book and then asked the monk to leave the book with him so that he could determine its worth. Since the dealer knew that Abbot Anastasius could tell him the value of the book, that evening the dealer took the book to Abbot Anastasius. The good abbot looked at the book, realized that it was his and that it had been stolen, but told the dealer only what the book was worth. The following day, the dealer told the monk what the book was worth, saying that he had asked Abbot Anastasius to look at it. The monk replied that he had decided not to sell the book, and then he returned the book to Abbot Anastasius and asked for his forgiveness.[51]

• Cher and Meryl Streep co-starred in the movie *Silkwood*. In a 1987 interview, Cher called Meryl "incredibly brave" and told about a night in Manhattan when the two saw a huge man mugging a woman: "Meryl screamed and ran straight at the man — who let go of the woman and ran straight at us! I thought we were going to be killed, but he ran between us and disappeared. We were both a wreck, but that's Meryl. She does what's right, no matter what." Meryl said, "I convince myself of my own courage. After I've played Isak Dinesen [in *Out of Africa*], I think I'm as brave as she is. I can fight lions — for a while. I stuff my straw in there, and I really believe I can scare the crows."[52]

• A thief went to Zen master Shichiri to rob him. Shichiri told the robber where his money was located, and then as the robber was leaving, he told the robber, "It's polite to say 'Thank you.'" The robber was so startled that in fact he said, "Thank you." A few days later, the robber was caught and taken to Shichiri, and the police asked Shichiri, "Did this man rob you?" Shichiri answered, "No. I gave him the money — he even thanked me for it." The robber did serve a prison term — for his other crimes — but after getting out of prison, he became Shichiri's disciple.[53]

• Country comedian Jerry Clower has many friends, including one man who planted one acre of cotton, came up with seven bales of cotton, and was put on trial for stealing cotton. Asked by the district attorney how he had gotten seven bales of cotton from only one acre, he replied, "I fertilize heavily."[54]

Day of Atonement

• Human beings are born with an Evil Inclination that lusts after forbidden things. On the Day of Atonement, Jews fast, neither eating nor drinking. According to the Palestinian Yoma VI, 4, on one Day of Atonement, Rabbi Haggai was ill, and Rabbi Mana visited him. Rabbi Haggai complained of thirst, and Rabbi Mana told him, "Seeing that you are sick, you may drink." However, Rabbi Haggai did not drink, instead saying, "The moment you permitted me to drink, my thirst disappeared."[55]

Death

• Mildred Frisby, reporter for the *Chicago American*, married Eddie Doherty of the *Chicago Tribune*. A few days after the marriage, she was assigned to cover the maiden voyage of a dirigible. However, before she and a photographer boarded the dirigible, her husband telephoned her. They spent some time together, and she ended up not boarding the dirigible. She arrived back at her newspaper to try to explain why she had missed the story, and city editor Eddie Mahoney stared at her and told her, "We've got you listed among the dead!" Shortly after takeoff, the dirigible had burst into flames, crashed, and killed 10 people, including the photographer for the *American*.[56]

• When Sharon Salzberg entered Burma and began to practice meditation, she experienced a great deal of discomfort, in part because of a persistent cough. She complained to the leader of the retreat, Sayama, who replied, "Well, I guess this will be good practice for when you die." This made Ms. Salzberg realize that spirituality is not just for when you feel well. It also made her realize that for many people, dying involves pain. After all, a dying body is a malfunctioning body, and dying people don't feel well.[57]

• In 1693, Zen Master Bankei knew that he was dying. When one of his disciples asked him to compose a traditional death poem, he replied, "I've lived for 72 years. I've been teaching people for 45. What I've been telling you and others every day during that time is my death verse. I'm not going to make another one now, before I die, just because everyone else does it."[58]

• The father of model/volleyball player Gabrielle Reece died in a plane crash. He was wearing a cross when he died, and that cross was found and delivered to Gabrielle. In memory of her father, she had a drawing of that cross tattooed on her ankle.[59]

• Elsie De Wolfe was an excellent interior decorator. When she was dying, she went to the hospital, where she was appalled by the decor. How appalled was she? She redecorated — and billed the hospital for her services.[60]

• Some European countries treat their cemeteries as living gardens. They are designed as much for the living as for the dead, and they include such things as picnic areas and jogging, bicycling, and hiking paths.[61]

• When Bankei, who later became a Zen master, was a child, he was so afraid of death that when he misbehaved, his parents were able to discipline him by lying down and pretending to die.[62]

Easter

• The story of Jesus' execution is gruesome and one must be careful how one tells small children about it. One little girl had attended services on Easter and was telling her mother about the preacher's description of the execution when she stopped and said, "You know, mama, I think that's a pretty scary story to be telling a little child like me."[63]

Education

• Bill Russell's grandfather had a lot of pride. He grew up in the Deep South in the pre-Civil Rights days, and people didn't care whether black kids went to school or not. In fact, his area didn't even have a school for black kids; therefore, Mr. Russell's grandfather decided that he would build a school for black kids. He paid in advance for the lumber at a mill, and then he drove a wagon out to the store to pick up the lumber. Unfortunately, the white man who owned the lumber mill didn't want to hand over the lumber. He told Mr. Russell's grandfather, "Negro kids don't need no school. They don't need to read to pick cotton." Mr. Russell's grandfather called everybody "Sir," and he said, "Okay, Sir. You can give me my money back." The man didn't want to do that, and he said, "Hell, there ain't no agreement with a Negro that a white man's got to respect." Mr. Russell's grandfather replied, "Well, Sir. Then you got three options. You can give me my lumber. You can give me my money. Or I can *kill* you." He got the lumber, he built the school for black kids, and he raised the teacher's first year's salary. As a Boston Celtic, Bill played 13 seasons, and he and the Celtics won 11 championships.[64]

• Allison lives in Minnesota and is educated at home — a process called homeschooling. Her parents are her teachers, and they are very creative at coming up with original ways to teach Allison. For example, when she was eight years old, Allison pretended to be a waitress during breakfast one day and wrote down each person's order, figured out the total cost of their meal, and made change from the money her mother gave her. The words she misspelled on the orders were added to her spelling list, and her father checked her math to make sure it was accurate. By the way, Allison remembers the first word she learned how to read. The word was "Fan," and it was a word in a story about a cow named "Fan." Also by the way, she likes to eat "ants on a log." To make this treat is easy: Put some peanut butter on a stick of celery, then put some raisins on the peanut butter. (Allison says, "Yummy.")[65]

• A young warrior started a fight with a peasant, but no matter what he did he could not defeat the peasant. Astonished, the young warrior asked the peasant how he had acquired such skill, and the peasant explained that he had been taught by an old master in the village. The young warrior visited the old master, but instead of listening and learning, the young warrior bragged loudly at great length about his accomplishments. The old master listened politely, but when he poured tea for the young warrior, he filled the teacup and then kept on pouring, causing the teacup to overflow and spill. Finally, the young warrior pointed out that no more would go into the teacup, and the old master replied, "The cup, young man, is much like your mind — so full that anything else put into it will only spill out."[66]

• To understand this anecdote, you must be aware that orthodox Jews believe that male Jews should keep their head covered. Orthodox Rabbi Joseph Kahaneman raised much money for Jewish schools. Once he went to a rich but fiercely anti-orthodox rich man to ask for money. The man looked at the rabbi, then said, "I'll give you money for your school provided that the students are forbidden to wear any kind of head covering at any time." "I agree," said Rabbi Kahaneman, and accepted the rich man's money. Soon afterward, a new Jewish Orthodox school opened: The B'nai B'rak School for Girls.[67]

• Abbot Anthony was talking with some brothers when a hunter saw them relaxing and enjoying themselves. The hunter disapproved and asked why they weren't out doing good works. Abbot Anthony answered by asking the hunter to draw his bow. The hunter did, then Abbot Anthony asked him to draw it tighter and tighter. Finally, the hunter said, "If I draw it any tighter, it will break. It is time to loosen the bow." Then Abbott Anthony said, "So it is with the work of God. If we push ourselves too much, we will break and become useless. At times, it is necessary to relax."[68]

• When the U.S. women's national soccer team won the first Women's World Cup in 1991, team member Julie Foudy thought that women's soccer would immediately become very popular in the United States. She was wrong, although later women's soccer did become much more popular. No one met the team at the airport, and when one of her Stanford professors learned what she had done, the professor said, "You won the World Cup? Oh. That's wonderful. Welcome back. Here is your final exam in human biology."[69]

• A cowardly warrior wished to be braver and better, so he sought advice from Japanese masters of the martial arts. However, they gave him advice that greatly surprised him: To be a braver and better warrior, study the tactics and methods of a successful businessperson. The warrior did so, and he discovered that the successful businessperson steadfastly faced problems and overcame them. After studying the tactics and methods of a successful businessperson, the warrior steadfastly faced problems and overcame them, and he became braver and better.[70]

• As a high school student, George Lucas, who grew up to make the *Star Wars* and *Indiana Jones* movies, seemed unremarkable, but an art teacher recognized the talent that was hidden inside him. The art teacher told young George's parents, "You have no idea what ability this boy has." By the way, when Francis Ford Coppola, a friend of *Star Wars* filmmaker George Lucas, directed *Apocalypse Now*, he included an in-joke. Early in the movie, an intelligence officer wears this name tag: "Col. G. Lucas."[71]

• A general in the Orient had an antique teacup that he greatly prized. One day, he was admiring it when it nearly slipped out of his hand, greatly alarming him. This made the general think: "I have been a general in battle after battle, often risking my life, yet never have I been as alarmed as I was when I nearly dropped this teacup. Why is this?" The general realized that he had become overly attached to the teacup, so he walked away, throwing the teacup over his shoulder and smashing it.[72]

• When British actress Dorothy Tutin first began to study acting, her mother wasn't sure how serious she was. However, when one day she came home from school, terribly upset because she felt she was lacking what was needed to become a great actress, her mother said, "If that's how you feel, then I have confidence in you. If you feel like that, that is how an artist should feel; I insist you go on and do it and work hard."[73]

• Rabbi Shlomo Carlebach didn't criticize people, but he was sometimes saddened by their behavior. Once he caught a student smoking marijuana, and he told the student, "Yisroel, if it would make you learn Torah better, I'd encourage it. But as it is, you end up falling asleep in class, so what's the point?" The student put out the marijuana cigarette, and he never smoked marijuana again.[74]

• A successful pro athlete can make quite a lot of money from endorsements, but these endorsements require a commitment of time. In 1998, tennis star Martina Hingis was favored to win the Grand Slam tournaments, but for six months she didn't win even one tournament. Why? She says, "I learned I should not make so many commercials the week before a Grand Slam."[75]

• Rabbi Gamaliel once told a servant, "Bring me something good." The servant went to the marketplace, then returned with a tongue. Gamaliel then told the servant, "Bring me something bad." The servant again went to the marketplace and returned with a tongue, then said to Gamaliel, "A tongue can be good or bad, depending on how it is used."[76]

• The Chofetz Chayim was against students pulling all-nighters; instead, he ordered that the lights be put out at midnight. He explained, "Whenever you have the desire to stay up all night to study, remember that this is a trick of the Evil Inclination. He wants you to go without sleep in order that you might be incapacitated for study altogether."[77]

• According to the Rabbi of Sadagora, we can learn about God from the inventions of Humankind. From a train, we can learn that "because of one second we can miss everything." From a telegraph, we can learn that "every word is counted and charged." And from a telephone, we can learn that "what we say here is heard there."[78]

• According to Isaac Bashevis Singer, who grew up in Poland, the first day that a Jewish child went to school was celebrated more joyously than the child's Bar Mitzvah. When a page of the Torah was set in front of the child, it was sprinkled with raisins and candy so that the child would associate learning with sweetness.[79]

• Panshan Baoji was people-watching in the marketplace. He saw a man who was buying wild boar and who told the butcher, "Give me a pound of the good stuff." The butcher smiled and said, "Which part here is not the good stuff?" This gave Panshan Baoji an insight: This moment of your life is part of the good stuff.[80]

• When David Schankula was attending high school in Kentucky, he and his friends discovered an old state law that said any student who requests it must be given a day off to attend the state fair. Because the law was still on the books, David and his friends requested and got a day off from school.[81]

• A man once challenged Hillel to convert him to Judaism — on condition that Hillel teach him all of the Torah while the man stood on one foot. Hillel responded, "What is hateful to you, do not do to your neighbor: this is the whole Torah. The rest is commentary; now go and study."[82]

• After getting his college education, Dave Herman became an offensive linesman for the New York Jets. This is how he made the decision to go pro: "At Michigan State, I majored in Agriculture and Economics, and from Economics, I learned there's no money in Agriculture."[83]

• Mulla Nasrudin once asked a group of people, "Would you like to acquire knowledge without study, good jobs without skills, and wealth without work?" The people eagerly crowded around Nasrudin and shouted, "Yes! Yes! Yes!" Nasrudin then said, "So would I."[84]

• Scott Adams' cartoon *Dilbert* can be educational — frequently, employees use it to educate their managers. Whenever a cartoon appropriate to their particular situation appears, employees clip it out, slip it under the office door of their manager, and then run away.[85]

• Dasui Fazhen, a 10th-century Zen master, was once asked, "How are you at the time when life-death arrives?" He answered, "When served tea, I take tea; when served a meal, I take a meal."[86]

• Michael Moore, director of *Roger and Me*, suggests that high school students start a club and make everyone a President because it will look good on their college applications.[87]

Fans

• Dr. Harold Carlson, coach of the University of Pittsburgh basketball team, once felt that the referees in Morgantown, the home of the West Virginia Mountaineers, were making way too many calls in favor of the home team, so he vigorously protested the calls, shouting, "That burns me up." Unfortunately, he said that one too many times, and a Mountaineer fan poured a bucket of water on him, saying, "That should cool you off."[88]

• Tennis star Anna Kournikova has quite a number of remarkable male fans. At the 1998 Australian Open, a couple of male fans dressed like her, couple with tennis dresses, breasts, and wigs with her trademark long braid. At one Australian Open, a group of male fans displayed a banner that bore this message: "Anna, will you marry me?" Ms. Kournikova asked mischievously, "Which one? Should I marry all of them?"[89]

• When he was in high school, *Star Trek* fan Jason Lighthall wanted to do something special for his yearbook photograph, so he dressed up in his Starfleet uniform for picture day.[90]

Fathers

• The World Wide Web has a number of interesting sites about health, including <livingto100.com>, which includes a questionnaire that it uses to calculate your expected lifespan. Jonathan Pond's nine-year-old daughter wanted to fill out the questionnaire, and thinking of an educational use of the questionnaire, he told her, "Fill it out as if you are doing everything bad for your health — drugs, booze, bad diet, no exercise, smoking, and so on." His daughter did, and she discovered that the Web site calculated that she would die at age 17.[91]

• When Steve Roberts asked Hale Boggs for permission to marry Cokie, his daughter, he was nervous. Fortunately, Mr. Boggs simply said, "Fine." Steve added because he is Jewish and Cokie is Catholic, "I know you think Cokie and I will have problems because of religion, but I think we can work them out." Mr. Boggs replied, "Yes, I do think you'll have problems, but not half as many problems as I'll have if I try to tell Cokie who to marry."[92]

• Mary Tyler Moore became a co-star on *The Dick Van Dyke Show* only after missing a chance to play Danny Thomas' daughter Terry on his show because, as Mr. Thomas said, "Nobody could believe that a daughter of mine would have a nose like yours."[93]

• Ed Sullivan committed a few bloopers in his day. He once asked vocalist Jack Jones, "Wasn't Alan Jones your father?" Jack replied, "He still is."[94]

Chapter 3: From Food to Medals

Food

• American author and chef Anthony Bourdain was not a vegetarian, but he was against fast food, and he wanted his two-and-a-half-year daughter to be against fast food. He and his wife even carried out against Ronald McDonald campaigns of the sort that the CIA calls black propaganda. For example, one day when he and his wife knew that their daughter was lying in bed still awake, they stood outside her door and carried out a campaign. His wife said, "Sssshhhh! She can hear us." He replied, "No, she's asleep." They then talked about Ronald McDonald being involved in the disappearance of a young child. His wife gasped, "Not another one!" He replied, "I'm afraid so. [The child s]tepped inside to get some fries and a Happy Meal, and hasn't been seen since. They're combing the woods ... checked out the Hamburglar's place — but, of course, they're focusing on Ronald again." And whenever Mr. Bourdain saw Ronald on TV or on a billboard, he said to his daughter, "Ronald smells bad. Kind of like ... poo! I'm not saying it rubs off on you or anything — if you get too close to him — but ...." Grossed out, his daughter said, "Ewwww."[95]

• One winter, Mulla Nasrudin made a bet with some friends that he could stay in the marketplace for an entire night without anything to warm him. The friends agreed that whoever won the bet would be treated to a meal by the loser. So Nasrudin stayed an entire night in the marketplace, with only a candle to keep him company. However, the following morning his friends said that he had lost the bet because he had been warmed by the candle. That evening, the friends arrived at Nasrudin's house to enjoy a meal, but Nasrudin kept them waiting and waiting because he said the soup was not warm yet. Finally, Nasrudin's friends went into the kitchen to find out why the soup still wasn't warm. There they saw a huge pot of soup being heated by a candle.[96]

• Despite his remarkable success as a filmmaker, George Lucas (of *Star Wars* and *Indiana Jones* fame) leads a simple lifestyle. He usually dresses in jeans, tennis shoes, and checked shirts, and when he invited actor Mark Hamill (who played Luke Skywalker) to dinner, they ended up eating at the local Taco Hut. Afterward, Mr. Hamill said, "I should have known that George wouldn't go to a place with tablecloths and waiters." By the way, the voice of Chewbacca, a tall, furry character in the *Star Wars* movies (Episodes 4, 5, and 6), is somewhat complex. The voice was created by combining the sounds made by a bear, a lizard, a seal, a tiger, and a walrus.[97]

• The Dalai Lama can be very open. Once, he toured Gethsemani Monastery in Kentucky. The monastery made its own cheeses and fruitcakes, and the Dalai Lama was offered some cheese. Later, he joked, "I was presented with a piece of the homemade cheese, which was very good, but really I wanted some cake! It was so unfortunate — really I was hoping someone would offer me some cake, but no one did!" The Dalai Lama was able to be happy without fruitcake, and some of his happiness came from being able to laugh at his desire for fruitcake.[98]

• As a child, Abbe Lane often visited her paternal grandmother for the weekend. Her grandmother was thrifty, and she found a subtle way of making young Abbe clean her plate — anything that Abbe didn't eat at breakfast appeared on her plate for lunch, anything that Abbe didn't eat at lunch appeared on her plate for dinner, and anything that Abbe didn't eat at dinner appeared on her plate for breakfast. Years after growing up, Ms. Lane says she orders small servings at restaurants out of a fear that if she doesn't clean her plate she will have to eat the leftovers at her next meal.[99]

• In 1947, the All American Girls Professional Baseball League went to Cuba for spring training. There they played several exhibition games against the Cuban women's team, Las Cubanas. However, on May Day, the players were not allowed to leave their hotel rooms because different Cuban political factions sometimes fought on that day and so the streets might not be safe. The only way the players could get food was by lowering baskets to Cuban boys playing in the street and paying them to load the baskets with food.[100]

• Mulla Nasrudin was hungry when he saw a group of travelers feasting by the side of the road. He sat down and joined them and began feasting on the bread, the fruits, the cheese, and the olives. The travelers began asking among themselves who the newcomer was and discovered that no one knew him, so they asked Nasrudin, "Whom do you know here?" Nasrudin replied, "I know the bread, the fruits, the cheese, and the olives."[101]

• *Los Angeles Times* columnist Meghan Daum once knew a morbidly obese man (he died of heart disease when he was around 50 years old). He used to go into a restaurant and eat several meals (15,000 calories) and drink a diet soda (1 calorie). His saving grace was that he was a man of wit: He would sometimes tell the server, "I'll have the left-hand side of the menu."[102]

• Mulla Nasrudin was very hungry and dipped all five fingers of his hand into a bowl of rice, although the etiquette of his time stated that one should get rice with only the thumb and the first two fingers. A bystander asked him, "Why are you eating with five fingers?" Nasrudin replied, "Because I don't have six fingers."[103]

• Is love of good food hereditary? Perhaps. Famous chef Jacques Pépin rewarded his small daughter the first time she stood up in her crib by giving her butter and caviar on bread. She ate it and requested, "Encore, Papa."[104]

• Explorers are sometimes creative with cooking, despite having few ingredients to work with. One Antarctic explorer made peas with just a hint of mint by squeezing a little mint-flavored toothpaste into a pot of peas.[105]

• Fat and happy lesbian humorist Laura Jimenez sometimes thinks about standing outside a Jenny Craig weight loss center while eating a turkey leg and wearing a T-shirt that says, "Jenny did this to me."[106]

Friends

• During a church lesson on friendship, a woman said, "This is a good lesson. Friends. I'm glad I've got so many." Jerry Clower asked her how many friends she had, and she replied, "I reckon I've got a thousand." Mr. Clower then asked her how many of her friends she would wake up at 2 a.m. if she needed help, and she said, "Oh, I don't know anybody I'd do that to." Hearing this, Mr. Clower said, "Lady, you ain't got a friend in the world. Not a single friend to your name."[107]

• A Gentile and a Jew were great friends. One day, the Gentile told the Jew, "My friend, thou art not a Jew but a Christian." The Jew replied, "My friend, these qualities which you see in me and call Christian, I see in you and call Jewish."[108]

Gays and Lesbians

• When gay teenager Paul Guilbert asked fellow gay teenager Aaron Fricke to their high school prom, Mr. Fricke replied, "OK, but I'll never have time to buy a gown." And at his high school commencement, gay teenager Aaron Fricke wore a pink triangle on his gown in memory of all the homosexuals who had been persecuted throughout history, including the homosexuals who had been forced to wear pink triangles in Nazi concentration camps.[109]

• Lois Hoxie, a lesbian, used to share an apartment with a gay man. For entertainment, she went to lesbian bars, while he went to gay bars. She wonders what the neighbors thought on Saturday nights when she and her gay friend came out of the house together all dressed up, then went to separate cars and said, "Good night. See you later."[110]

• A couple of reporters for the sleazy tabloids once piled into a taxi and told the driver to drop them off at a place where they could meet women. Unfortunately for them, they had a gay cabbie with a sense of humor. He dropped them off at a disco for lesbians.[111]

• Some gay men choose funny ways to come out to their parents. One gay man told his father, "Dad, I'm gay, and either that frosted plastic chandelier goes or I go."[112]

Gifts

• On September 20, 1973, Billie Jean King and Bobby Briggs met in a tennis match played in the Astrodome in Houston, Texas. The match came about because of the braggadocio of Mr. Briggs, who enjoyed making outrageous bets and playing matches in which he was handicapped by carrying a heavy suitcase in one hand or by holding a leash chained to a dog as he played. In this case, the 55-year-old Briggs challenged a woman tennis pro who was 25 years younger than he. The match was filled with hoopla. Mr. Briggs entered the stadium in a cart pulled by six beautiful women, while Ms. King entered while riding on a chair carried by five handsome men. Before the match, the two competitors exchanged gifts. Mr. Briggs gave the "girl" a lollipop, while Ms. King gave the male chauvinist a piglet. Of course, Ms. King defeated Mr. Briggs in a match televised in 36 countries — she also won $100,000 in prize money.[113]

• Once a visitor came to see Mulla Nasrudin and brought him a gift of a duck, which Nasrudin accepted happily and used to make duck soup for his visitor. Although the visit was very enjoyable, it led to a problem for Nasrudin, because soon many more visitors came to his house for hospitality, announcing that they were friends of the man who had given Nasrudin the duck. Finally, Nasrudin decided that he had to stop such pushy visitors when the "friend of a friend of a friend of the man who gave you the duck" arrived at his house. So Nasrudin sat the man at his dinner table, then served him warm water in a soup bowl. The shocked visitor asked, "What is this?" Nasrudin replied, "This is the soup of the soup of the soup of the duck."[114]

• *Guardian* columnist Leo Hickman once made a list of 10 things that he could not live without. They include a toothbrush, a mobile phone, and a Swiss army penknife. However, the most valuable thing that he owns and cannot live without happens to be a gift. He writes, "I'm a shameless Prince fan, and I would rather rub swine flu in my eyes than be forced to give up the plectrum the world's greatest performer handed to me during a gig when I was 14 years old. This, then, is my most treasured possession of all." By the way, a plectrum is a device for plucking the strings of a musical instrument such as a guitar.[115]

• Frederick Varley was a good artist and a kind man. When famed photographer Yousuf Karsh was taking Mr. Varley's portrait, Mr. Karsh's second wife, Estrellita, looked through a pile of his works of art. She was impressed by a drawing that he had made — it was "only a spontaneous quick sketch and yet vividly alive." Mr. Varley gave it to her, and the Karshes hung it in their home.[116]

• In one episode of *Mr. Ed*, Zsa Zsa Gabor played her usual glamorous self, and asked that a full-length mink coat be rented for her to wear as part of her costume. Later, she drove off with the mink (which was worth $10,000) in her car and had to be stopped at the front gate of the studio: "I'm sorry, dahling," she said. "But most of the studios give me coats like this as gifts!"[117]

• As a Cardinal in Venice, Angelo Giuseppe Roncalli (later he became Pope John XXIII) once was shocked that a priest had given only 100 lira (a very small amount of money) to a poor person. He said, "A gift must be of some use," and advised that the priest should have given the poor person at least 1,000 lira.[118]

• Native American beadwork can be very complex. Contemporary Native American Dale Tex, a member of the Western Mono tribe, once made a belt for his wife, Julie — the belt was made of 18,000 beads![119]

• Artist Ed Burein once gave his friend Will Rogers a stuffed calf. This gift allowed Mr. Rogers to be indoors and still practice his roping.[120]

Good Deeds

• When Zen master Hakuin was a young Zen student, he learned that hidden virtue is rewarded. He was traveling with two older monks; all three travelers were carrying baggage. While he walked, Hakuin meditated. One of the older Zen monks pleaded that he was ill and asked Hakuin to carry his baggage for him. Hakuin agreed. The other monk then decided to take advantage of Hakuin by claiming that he also was ill and asking Hakuin to carry his baggage, too. Heavily loaded, Hakuin meditated while carrying all the baggage until the three monks reached the boat on which they would travel. Exhausted, Hakuin slept for a long time. When he awoke, he was surprised that the boat had traveled through a storm. While the other monks had been terrified by the storm, become seasick, and vomited, Hakuin had slept peacefully.[121]

• Even though pro football player Brian Piccolo was deathly ill, he snuck out of his patient's room for a while to visit a small girl who had broken her neck and had only a short time to live. Not long after, Mr. Piccolo died. Mr. Piccolo's friendship with running back Gale Sayers is well known. Accepting an award at a Pro Football Writers Dinner, Mr. Sayers stated that the award should have gone to Mr. Piccolo, who Mr. Sayers said showed more courage battling the illness that would kill him than Mr. Sayers showed on the football field.[122]

• Art Linkletter was once stopped by a man who insisted he had gone to school with him in Moosejaw, Canada. Actually, although Mr. Linkletter had been born there, he had moved when he was little to San Diego, California, where he went to school. However, because the man's family was with him, Mr. Linkletter was polite and pretended to have gone to school with the man in Moosejaw, Canada.[123]

• R' Leibele of Vilna used to stand in front of his home every Friday morning, looking for a poor person who could not afford to celebrate the Sabbath properly. When he saw such a person, he would call out that he needed a worker. The poor person would help the good Rabbi for a few hours, then R' Leibele would pay the person and urge the person to get ready to celebrate the Sabbath.[124]

• In 1977, many of Lily Tomlin's young fans waited in the winter cold so that they could buy front-row tickets to her one-woman Broadway show *Appearing Nightly*. She surprised them by appearing in character as Mrs. Beasley, who wore a 1940s Red Cross volunteer uniform and gave them coffee and doughnuts.[125]

Husbands and Wives

• At one time, Elizabeth Taylor was married to John W. Warner, a Senator from Virginia. After a trip to a Virginia oil field, Senator Warner was thirsty, so he stopped at a tiny country store to ask for a glass of water. However, the proprietress denied his request, saying, "We're running a business here. We've got Coke, Sprite, and 7-Up. Take your pick." Aghast, Senator Warner said, "You don't understand. I'm Senator John Warner and I want a glass of water." This did not impress the proprietress. Then one of the Senator's aides said to her, "You don't know this man. He's married to Elizabeth Taylor." This did impress her. She replied, "Well, then, he can have all the water he wants."[126]

• American artist Benjamin West became engaged to Elizabeth Shewell before he left the United States to study art in Europe. Although he was away for many years, Ms. Shewell never forgot him. When Mr. West's father decided to travel to England to see him, Mr. West asked him to bring Ms. Shewell with him. Unfortunately, Ms. Shewell's brother opposed the marriage, and he locked her up to keep her from going to England. It was Benjamin Franklin, always a resourceful man, who arranged her escape and provided a rowboat for her to reach the ship that would take her to England and her fiancé so they could be married.[127]

• Catherine Shipley was both a Quaker and a character. In the days when women wore bustles, she and her husband attended a party. Unfortunately, Kate couldn't find a dress with a bustle, so she tied a hot water bottle around her waist. Back home after the party, she and her husband began to get ready for bed, and her husband noticed the hot water bottle. Kate asked if he minded her using it as a bustle, and he replied, "No, of course not, but I did wonder what I heard gurgling all evening."[128]

• The ancient rabbis were against polygamy. They told a story of a man with two wives: one old and one young. While he was asleep, his young wife plunked out his grey hairs so that he would appear to be young. However, his old wife plunked out his black hairs so that he would appear to be old. Very quickly, the man became bald.[129]

• The wife of one of his enemies once dumped a pail of water over the head of Rabbi Levi Isaac. He went to the synagogue and prayed, "O Lord, God of Israel, do not punish the good woman. She must have done this at the command of her husband and is therefore to be commended as a loyal wife."[130]

• At the end of a marriage counseling session, a wife put on her coat and asked her husband whether the coat made her look fat. He replied, "No, but your rear end does." The marriage counselor asked the husband to remain a while longer for some additional counseling.[131]

• Jonathan Edwards sometimes preached gloom and doom, but his wife was always happy in her piety. People said about Mrs. Edwards that she had learned a shorter way to Heaven than her husband.[132]

• Red Skelton once asked fellow comedian Frank Morgan if he knew his wife. Mr. Morgan joked, "Of course, I know her — and love her. You rascal, I'm just waiting for you to pass away."[133]

Illnesses and Injuries

• In the old days, people believed in the healing powers of *kemeiyot* — religious texts written on parchment. One person who felt that this practice was a superstition was Rabbi Yechezkel Landau, who only once gave a *kemeiyah*: He gave it to an ill woman. Convinced that she was dying, the woman was wasting away for no apparent reason. Because the ill woman believed that only a *kemeiyah* from the rabbi could save her, Rabbi Landau obtained a piece of blank parchment and then rolled it up in a cloth. He then gave it to the woman's husband, telling him to tell his wife to wear the cloth around her neck for 30 days and then unwrap it and look at the parchment. If there was no writing on the parchment, that meant that she would be cured. The woman followed the Rabbi's orders; after 30 days, she looked at the parchment, saw no writing on it, and immediately began to get better. Soon she was healthy again.[134]

• As a small boy, comedian Louis Nye was very thin, and his Jewish mother took him to an Irish physician who said that to fatten up her son she needed to serve him bacon. This was very shocking because kosher bacon was unknown. However, his mother asked advice from his grandmother, who unhesitatingly recommended that for the boy's health she should follow the doctor's advice. His mother therefore purchased new kitchenware so that she wouldn't cook and serve bacon on her kosher kitchenware. Whenever she fried bacon for her son, all three of them — grandmother, mother, and young son — used newspapers to waft the smell of frying bacon out of the kitchen window. (By the way, the bacon worked — Louis was a healthy-looking boy at his bar mitzvah.)[135]

• Sometimes, nurses ask silly questions. When Quaker humorist Tom Mullen was in a hospital, he was standing up when he suddenly felt dizzy. He managed to buzz the nurses' station before he passed out, and when the nurse arrived, he was lying on the floor, semi-conscious, trying to get up. The nurse looked down at him and then asked, "May I help you?" Mr. Mullen wishes today that he had been conscious enough to reply, "No, I'm just crawling about at 2 a.m. looking for loose change."[136]

• Julie Krone was racing when another jockey rode his horse into her horse. Her horse's knees buckled, and Ms. Krone fell off. Looking up, she saw another horse running straight at her. The horse kicked her in the chest. Because the pain was so bad, all she could think was, "Pass out. Please pass out." Nine months and two operations later, she was back on the track, racing.[137]

• Female jockey Mary Bacon once suffered a serious concussion that left her unconscious and fighting for her life. Her mother sat with her, and a pleasant-looking man stopped by each morning. Eventually, her mother asked who the pleasant-looking man was. The hospital floor supervisor answered, "He's the undertaker." (Eventually, Ms. Bacon recovered and raced again.)[138]

• In his later years, Pope John Paul II was ill or injured several times. In 1994, while getting out of the shower he fell and broke his leg. Immediately, he was rushed to a Catholic teaching hospital, where he had been admitted five times previously. He joked to the officials at the hospital, "You have to admire my loyalty."[139]

• Elite gymnasts work very hard, and they do get physically tired as well as physically injured. When elite gymnast Kerri Strug had to get bone scans on her shins, she kept falling asleep during the scans, thus ruining them and being forced to start them again.[140]

• A nurse came in to give a patient a shot and asked him in which arm he wanted it. The patient — who disliked shots — thought for a moment and then said, "In *your* left arm, please."[141]

Insults

• A person was introduced to a deaf man. Not knowing much about deaf people, the person wrote "Can you read?" on a piece of paper, then he handed it to the deaf person. The deaf person read the question and was insulted by its ignorance, so he wrote back, "No, can you write?" By the way, one problem that deaf people have is trying to lip read the words of a person with a foreign accent.[142]

• Groucho Marx once belonged to a theatrical club. However, after a fellow member complained about the quality of the members the club was getting, Groucho decided to resign, so he sent a telegram to the club, saying: "Please accept my resignation. I don't want to belong to any club that would have me as a member."[143]

• Jackie Robinson feuded with sportswriter Mike Gaven. One day, when Mr. Gaven entered the Dodger dugout, Mr. Robinson told him, "You sports writers are always wrong." Mr. Gaven replied, "You mean like when we voted you Most Valuable Player last year?"[144]

• English entertainer Joyce Grenfell made a habit of being on time for appointments. Once, when an editor was late for a meeting with her, she telephoned his office and asked, "Is he *usually* unpunctual?"[145]

Language

• Janette Porter was the daughter of a preacher. While she was in elementary school in the early part of the 20th century, a classmate whispered to her that she had just had an evil thought and asked what she should do. Janette whispered back, "Just think about flowers ... and music ... and JESUS." Joy at finding exactly the right word to say made her say that word much too loudly, and her teacher and most of her classmates were shocked to hear the preacher's daughter "curse." As punishment, she had to stand in the corner of the classroom for an hour.[146]

• The parents of a student at Sidcot School became upset and complained, saying that a teacher had cursed at their son when he had lost a wallet. The Head of the school investigated the matter and discovered that lost property was turned over to a teacher named Helen Hunt. When the boy reported losing his wallet, he had been told, "Go to Helen Hunt for it."[147]

• The language old-time muledrivers used was something awesome to behold. One muledriver stopped to invite his frontier preacher to climb aboard for a ride. Unfortunately, the muledriver was quickly forced to disinvite the preacher — as long as the preacher was around, the mules didn't understand a word the muledriver said.[148]

• In one game, the Seattle Supersonics were trailing Vancouver by nine points at halftime. Later, Supersonic player Vin Baker was asked what coach George Karl had told the team in his halftime talk. Mr. Baker replied, "I'm a minister's son. I don't repeat those kinds of things."[149]

Medals

• Cathy Rigby was lucky to have good coaches when she began to study gymnastics in the early 1960s, because there weren't that many around. In fact, Muriel Grossfeld, one of the top American gymnasts of the 1950s and 1960s, said, "When I was competing, none of the best girls had coaches. We all trained ourselves." Fortunately for Ms. Rigby, Bob Marquette, a 1930s gymnastics champion, had started a girls gymnastics club in Long Beach, California, near her home. Why did he do this when they were so rare? He explained, "I started a girls' gymnastic club because they're always being put down. Boys have so much going for them in sports — football, basketball, baseball." Ms. Rigby's training paid off when she became the first American woman to win a medal in international competition: a silver medal on balance beam at the 1970 Worlds Games held in Yugoslavia.[150]

• Svetlana Boginskaya has a lot of pride. At her very first gymnastics competition, she won a second-place medal. She was so angry that she had not won first place that as soon as she was home, she threw the medal away.[151]

Chapter 4: From Media to Priests and Popes

Media

• At the *Chicago Herald-Examiner*, John J. "Jack" McPhaul once worked with a female reporter who was dedicated to meeting deadlines. Once, they were working together on a murder case. They waited for a coroner to finish his work on the murder victim so they could report on the findings. Their deadline for the first edition was fast approaching, and growing impatient she walked into the coroner's office. A moment later, the coroner appeared and beckoned to Mr. McPhaul. Two bodies were lying down. One was the murder victim; the other was the female reporter. Mr. McPhaul asked what had happened, and the coroner replied, "She tapped me on the shoulder, and when I turned it was just in time to catch her. Out like a light. Guess the job was a little messier than she had expected." The female reporter regained consciousness, looked at Mr. McPhaul, and said, "Jack McPhaul, if you ever tell a soul, I'll kill you."[152]

• Reporters for the tabloids play dirty tricks on each other, such as calling an opposing newspaper with a bogus news tip. For example, a reporter will be sent out to investigate a place where a major celebrity is supposed to be recuperating from a life of excess. The reporter will drive for hours, only to find out that the address given by the tipster is that of a desert shack no celebrity would ever live in. In addition, reporters for the tabloids have to deal with a lot of crazy people. At the height of the excitement generated by the O.J. Simpson trial, a wacko called the *Star* and demanded $300,000 for an exclusive psychic interview with a dog named Kato.[153]

• As an employee at the *Chicago Sun-Times*, Roger Ebert was one of the reporters who spent a lot of time at Billy Goat's and at Riccardo's. Reporters from the *Chicago Daily News* spent much time at both places, too. Billy Goat's was a bar, and Riccardo's was an Italian restaurant. When Riccardo's was sold, a *Chicago Sun-Times* reporter interviewed the seller, who said that he had enjoyed being the owner of the restaurant, with one exception: "On Friday nights, they let the animals out of the zoo." John McHugh, a *Daily News* reporter, read the article, and then told Roger, "Ebert, he means us."[154]

• Many males did not accept celebrated female jockey Julianne Krone early in her career. One sportswriter followed her winning career for an entire year before deciding that she was as good as — or better than — the male jockeys. The headline for his article about her read, "Too Damn Bad She's a Girl."[155]

Mishaps

• In 1975, Jim White borrowed a skateboard from a friend while preparing for a surfing competition in Hawaii and then badly injured his leg in a fall while skating. For a few weeks, he could not walk — not even with crutches. For two months, he was in a full-leg cast. Of course, he was bored, and he watched a lot of television. He also borrowed a guitar and "started trying to learn guitar for two hours each afternoon, during that period when there were no game shows or reruns of *Star Trek* or *Dark Shadows* on." This worked out for him, as he has written many, many songs and has become a recording artist. What would have happened to him if he had not broken his leg? He asks, "I likely would have gone to Hawaii and been blown out in my first heat (the Hawaiians' skills were far superior to mine), come home and spent the next few decades taking odd jobs and trying to figure out how to make a living as a professional surfer. So my question is this, which was a better borrowed object for me: the skateboard, or the guitar?" His debut album is titled *Wrong-Eyed Jesus: The Mysterious Tale of How I Shouted*.[156]

• As a teenager, Dorothy Hamill sometimes got upset at important competitions, but fortunately her father was present to help her calm down. At the 1974 World Championships, young Dorothy skated onto the ice to perform her free skating program, but she heard the crowd booing, so she burst into tears and skated off the ice to her father. He pointed out that the boos weren't for her — the fans were booing the low scores the judges had given the previous skater. Dorothy recovered enough to win the silver medal. At the 1976 Olympic Games, young Dorothy again became upset and started crying, this time when she saw a sign that said, "Dorothy, Wicked Witch of the West." Fortunately, her father explained that the sign was a complimentary reference to *The Wizard of Oz,* in which Dorothy shows great courage in combating the Wicked Witch of the West. This time, young Dorothy won the gold medal.[157]

• One of filmmaker John Waters' friends used to work at a movie theater, which meant that he constantly had to pick up the telephone and answer the question, "What's playing today?" The friend reports that the most embarrassing title he ever had to say on the telephone was *Eu te Amo*, which is Brazilian Portuguese for "I love you." When he told them the title of the movie, some people were shocked and asked, "I beg your pardon?" Other people cursed him, and one person told him, "I *hate* you," before hanging up the telephone.[158]

• Bette Midler learned how to sew early in life, which meant that as an eighth grader, she was able to wear a copy of Satin Surrender (original by Frederick's of Hollywood) to her school in Honolulu. By the way, poi is a common food on the Hawaiian Islands, and it is eaten by dipping your fingers into it. One of raised-on-Hawaii Bette Midler's more egregious social errors overseas came during a party when she mistook a bowl of haggis for poi.[159]

• Even preachers sometimes make mistakes. Church of Christ preacher W.A. Bradfield was closing a sermon with a call to the altar and was doing his best to call the unrepentant to come to the altar and repent: "Oh, why don't you come? You daddies, for your children's sake, why don't you come? Oh, why don't you come, you husbands, for your wives' sake? Oh, for heaven's sake, why don't you come? Oh, why in the h*ll don't you come?"[160]

• Art Bray once performed the funeral of a woman who died during the wintertime. The next summer, during a heat wave, he ran into the woman's daughter and without thinking, asked, "How is your mother standing the heat?" Shocked, the woman's daughter asked, "Oh, Pastor, is that where you think she went?"[161]

• After some transsexuals were beaten up, gay author Joel Perry joined a protest against such violence. As part of the protest, the activists wore old shirts so that slogans could be painted on them. Mr. Perry requested that "Stop the Hate" be printed on his T-shirt. Unfortunately, after the protest march, he discovered that written on his T-shirt was the slogan "Stop the Hat."[162]

• At her all-female college, Katherine Hepburn played men's roles in the plays the theater department put on. During one play, she put a hand in her pants pocket, sat down, and couldn't get her hand out again.[163]

Money

• Old-time newspapers used copyboys to run articles (copy) from the reporters to an editor. At the *Chicago Sun-Times*, one of the copyboys was known as Milton the Copyboy. Just one of his many jobs was to run errands for the reporters. For example, they would send him out to buy a drink. Of course, drinking was not permitted at the newspaper, but Milton would camouflage the drink by putting it in a paper coffee cup and by also bringing sugar and cream. One day, a mystery was discovered. Several hundred empty envelopes were found in the trash near Milton the Copyboy's home. All of the envelopes were addressed to Ann Landers. A post office employee brought up this matter to *Sun-Times* editor James Hoge, who then brought the matter up to Milton the Copyboy. It turned out that Milton had been stealing the quarters that people were sending in as payment for Ann Landers' pamphlet "Petting: When Does It Go Too Far?" Milton the Copyboy was fired, even though he believed that he had done a good deed in the world: "Hundreds of kids can thank me that they were conceived."[164]

• On 2 December 1975, a Carson City, Nevada, business man named Harold Hess was given a parking ticket even though he told the police officer that he had tried to put a coin in the parking meter but could not because the parking meter was frozen. He even used a dime to demonstrate to the police officer that the parking meter would not work because it was frozen. However, the police officer merely shrugged, said, "That's not my problem," and walked away. Mr. Hess decided to pay the parking ticket, and he walked into the courthouse the next day carrying a lump of ice in which was frozen both the parking ticket and the money to pay the parking ticket. The justice asked, "How am I supposed to get that out of there?" Mr. Hess shrugged, said, "That's not my problem," and walked away.[165]

• When Susan Butcher started to enter sled dog racing contests, such as the 1,049-mile-long Iditarod Trail Sled Dog Race in Alaska, she wanted a sponsor to help cover some of the costs. Long-time musher John Redington, aka the Father of the Iditarod, helped by arranging a publicity stunt for her. He convinced a couple of radio stations to film her as she chopped a hole in the ice, then jumped in while wearing a bathing suit. Supposedly, this stunt — which worked — was to show how mushers stay clean. This is not to say that Ms. Butcher never had trouble with sponsors. Once, she expected to sign with a sponsor, so she charged $6,000 of dog food. Unfortunately, the sponsor decided not to make the deal, so she had to pay back the loan $10 and $25 at a time.[166]

• The Zen master Mokusen Hiki visited a rich man, who was very miserly. He held out a closed hand to the miser, and asked, "If my hand were always like this, what would you call it?" The miser answered, "Deformed." Mokusen Hiki then held out a hand that was opened wide and asked, "If my hand were always like this, what would you call it?" The miser again answered, "Deformed." Mokusen Hiki then said to the rich man, "If you understand this, you are a happy rich man." The miser thought for a long time, then changed his ways. When there was a reason to be thrifty, he was thrifty. When there was a reason to be generous, he was generous.[167]

• Izel Harif (died 1873) was the rabbi of Slonim. Once he went to a rich man to collect money for the building of a school, but the rich man refused to donate any money. This did not surprise Rabbi Harif, who knew that the rich often donate money out of fear. Thus, a rich man who fears becoming poor will donate money to help the poor, and a rich man who fears becoming ill will donate money to help the ill. Since this particular rich man was stupid and unlikely ever to suffer from a thirst for learning, the good rabbi knew that he was unlikely to donate to the building of a school.[168]

• In the early days, professional marathon swimmers made little money competing in their sport. Professional marathon swimmer Diana Nyad once complained, "I once swam a 10-mile race and won $35." Even worse, Ms. Nyad and other professional marathon swimmers went to a competition in Buenos Aires, Argentina. They had heard that the winner would receive $3,000, but when they arrived, they discovered that they were mistaken. The winner would receive 3,000 pesos, which at the time were worth about 12 cents.[169]

• Rabbi Shlomo Carlebach once bought a soda to go that cost 50 cents, handed the cashier $2, and told her to keep the change. A friend told him that when you order to go, you don't need to tip, and you certainly don't tip $1.50 for a 50-cent soda. Rabbi Shlomo smiled and said, 'I know, I know. But I'm trying to make up for *unzer tierla yiddalach* [our sweet Jews] who don't give tips, and consequently make a *chilul hashem* [defame God's name]."[170]

• Long-distance telephone bills used to be much higher than they are now. In the 1970s, young American gymnast Leslie Russo was competing in South Africa. She got homesick, so she called home —

and her family paid $92 for the first three minutes. After that experience, her mother told her, "Don't call — write!"[171]

• A man gained admittance to the very wealthy Rothschild by saying he could save him 500,000 rubles. When Rothschild asked him how he could do this, the man replied, "I have heard that you are giving your daughter a dowry of 1,000,000 rubles. I am here to tell you that I am willing to marry her for only 500,000 rubles."[172]

Motivation

• Gymnast Dominique Dawes believes in staying motivated. During the trials for the 1996 Olympic Games, she kept inspirational quotations scattered throughout her hotel room. The quotations included these: "Don't make excuses. Make good." "Who dares nothing need hope for nothing." "Great visions often start with small dreams."[173]

• Shannon Miller's mother helped motivate her to learn new gymnastics skills. For example, her mother would promise that if Shannon learned a new skill, she would get a Cabbage Patch doll or she could choose the menu for dinner.[174]

Music

• Comedian Steve Martin is a master of the clawhammer style of playing the banjo. A serious musician, he has played with many bluegrass greats, including Earl Scruggs. Mr. Scruggs' wife, Louise, once happened to mention that each Gibson banjo that the Scruggs owned was worth $200,000. Mr. Martin, who has a collection of vintage banjos — among them, two Depression-era Gibson Florentines and a Gibson Granada — immediately thought that he perhaps he should get them insured. He called George Gruhn, who is a vintage instrument dealer in Nashville, and said, "George, I hear these Florentines are worth some money." Indeed, they are; for example, the Florentines owned by Mr. Scruggs are worth the $200,000 Louise mentioned — or more — because they are associated with Mr. Scruggs. Mr. Martin then asked about his own vintage banjos. Mr. Gruhn said, "With your name attached? About $8,000."[175]

• All too often, people want to hear old hits, not the new music that a band has created. The Fixx creatively solved this problem when their album *Elemental* was new. Band members went on tour and played most or all of their new album before playing their old hits. Fixx lead singer Cy Curnin thinks that is fair. The band members get to play their new music, and the fans get to hear the old hits. And, with luck, the new album will have a few songs that eventually become old hits because of their exposure in live concerts. Mr. Curnin said, "You've just got to be ballsy these days; otherwise, you don't get anywhere."[176]

• Jazz singer Billie Holiday wore a gardenia in her hair while she performed. Early in her career, she had been ironing her hair in preparation for a performance, and she burned it, leaving a bare spot on her scalp that she covered with a gardenia. She liked the look of the gardenia in her hair, so she continued to wear one even after her hair grew back to normal again.[177]

Names

• Major-league pitcher Christy Mathewson became known as "Big 6" because of his height. He stood 6-foot-2 at a time when that height was not as common as it is now. Someone said, "That's the biggest six-footer you ever saw," and Mr. Mathewson got a nickname. Someone once mailed a letter whose envelope simply had pasted on it a big number 6 that had been cut out of a newspaper headline. The letter was delivered to Mr. Mathewson.[178]

• Andrew Jackson was as tough as hickory, a fact that gave him his nickname. Old Hickory was known for having things done his way — or no way at all. As President, he vetoed more bills than all of the Presidents before him put together had vetoed. When he died, a dignitary asked a field man who had worked for Mr. Jackson whether Old Hickory would go to Heaven. The field hand replied, "He will, sir, if he wants to."[179]

• The doctrine of papal infallibility was promulgated in 1870, and the press was much interested in this doctrine, regularly asking bishops about it. After James Gibbons (1834-1921) became a bishop, and on returning home from a trip to Rome where he had met the Pope, he was asked about papal infallibility. He replied, "All I know is that he kept referring to me as Jibbons." (Italians often pronounce the letter G as the letter J.)[180]

• When Jackie Joyner-Kersee was born, her grandmother said that when she grew up, she would be the first lady of something. That's why she was named after then-First Lady Jackie Kennedy.[181]

• At the 1984 Olympic Games, Kathy Johnson's teammates called her "Grandma" because at age 24, she was the oldest member of the United States women's gymnastics team.[182]

• Michelle Kwan's father, Danny, is a fan of music by the Beatles. In fact, he liked the Beatles' song "Michelle" so much that he named his second daughter after it.[183]

• Sportswriter Franz Lidz, in collaboration with his wife, Maggie, named their daughters "Gogo" and "Daisy Daisy."[184]

Olympics

• The night before playing in the championship game as a goaltender on the United States women's hockey team at the 1998 Nagano Olympic Games, Sarah Tueting found it difficult to get to sleep. Seeing a bowl of apples in her room, she picked up an apple and hurled it at the middle of a wall, creating a big splat! She kept on hurling apples until she ran out, although her roommate told her, "Get away from me!" The apple-throwing incident must have had a therapeutic effect — she and her team won the championship game and the gold medal the following day.[185]

• Before gymnastics practices, two of Olga Korbut's teammates sometimes used to hold on to her hands and feet and swing her like a jump rope. Before the 1972 Olympic Games in Munich, Olga was motivated to succeed. In fact, a 1970 entry in her diary stated, "1972, Munich, Olympic Games — 1st place."[186]

People with Handicaps

• Often, the first thing two deaf people do when they go to a nice restaurant is to remove the centerpiece so they have an unobstructed view of each other's hands. (In addition, they make certain that the restaurants they go to are well lit.)[187]

• A blind singer received the first of many standing ovations in his career. After he had been told that he had received a standing ovation, he asked, "What is a standing ovation?"[188]

Practical Jokes

• Among filmmaker John Waters' many collectables are three two-foot-high dolls with hair that you can style. Mr. Waters has named the dolls "Tiny," "Kim," and "Kathy." Although he takes cares of the dolls, occasionally he would return home and find that some of his friends had used makeup to simulate bruises and black eyes on the dolls so that they looked like they had been abused.[189]

• As a part of his work as a master of special effects in the movies and on TV, Wah Ming Chang created a gorilla suit. At a party, he once scared a guest, who discovered what seemed to be a gorilla sitting on a toilet.[190]

Preachers

• An old minister wanted a new church annex to be built. He listened as his 12 deacons argued about the advantages and disadvantages of the new annex, then said, "You have heard all the good reasons why the new annex should be built, and all the unreasonable things said against the new annex. Now it is time for a vote. All those in favor of building the new annex will so signify by saying 'aye.' Six deacons said, "Aye." The old preacher continued, "All those against building the new annex will so signify by saying 'I resign.'"[191]

• A preacher in a small-town church was offered a job at twice the salary preaching in a big-city church. A member of the congregation, wondering whether the preacher would accept the job, stopped by the preacher's house and knocked on the door. The preacher's daughter answered the door, and he asked her where the preacher was. She replied, "He's on his knees praying for divine guidance about whether to accept the job offer." He then asked, "Where's your mother?" The preacher's daughter replied, "She's upstairs packing."[192]

• Mr. Betterton, an actor, believed that the theaters would soon be empty if actors spoke like preachers. Conversely, if preachers spoke like actors, the churches would soon be full. When asked why this was so, since preachers speak about real things, and actors speak about imaginary things, Mr. Betterton replied, "My lord, I can assign but one reason — we players speak of things imaginary as though they were real, and too many of the clergy speak of things real as though they were imaginary."[193]

• Alvin K. Klotz used to speak before many Protestant churches, and the churches used variations of the Lord's Prayer. Some churches used, "Forgive us our debts," others used, "Forgive us our trespasses," and still others used, "Forgive us our sins." Therefore, before reciting the Lord's Prayer, Mr. Klotz used to say, "It would help me greatly to know if you are debtors, trespassers, or sinners."[194]

• Marshall Keeble was a black Church of Christ preacher who stood up for his beliefs. A white man once told him in Tennessee, "You preach like this anymore, you'll leave town or we'll kill you." Preacher Keeble replied, "I kissed my wife before I left Nashville, Tennessee. My Lord died for me. I'd just as soon die for him in Lexington, Tennessee, as anywhere else." Mr. Keeble continued to preach.[195]

• While preaching at a church in Bentley Creek, Pennsylvania, Wesleyan pastor William Woughter had the misfortune of being bothered by a fly that buzzed around him, then flew straight into his mouth, causing him to gag until he was finally forced to swallow the fly. Pastor William then looked at the congregation and said, "That reminds me of the scripture, 'I was a stranger and you took me in.'"[196]

• June Cerza Kolf tells this story: At her family reunion held in California, an earthquake struck as the family members attended church. Afterwards, one of the family members, who was new to California, told the pastor, "I've been to a lot of church services in my life, but I can honestly say this was the most moving one I've ever attended."[197]

• Rev. Ronald J. Mohnickey once celebrated Mass on a very hot summer day at a nearby church in Steubenville, Ohio. A smiling woman said to him after the liturgy, "I am so happy when you celebrate Mass here! When you come here, they always turn on the air conditioning because you sweat so much!"[198]

Priests and Popes

• Papal Nuncio Angelo Giuseppe Roncalli, who was later to be Pope John XXIII, once met the Chief Rabbi of Paris at a reception. They talked together for a long time, and when they were summoned to dinner, they were confronted with the dilemma of who would walk through the door to the dining room first. Nuncio Roncalli motioned for the Rabbi to go first, saying, "The Old Testament before the New."[199]

• Father Bob Perella was known as the priest to the stars. Frequently, he hung around with Perry Como. One day Father Bob and Mr. Como met Vic Damone, who was also with a priest. When Father Bob asked Mr. Damone what was up, he replied, "If you can make Perry such a big star, you must have a pretty good connection. I figured I'd use somebody from the same agency."[200]

• Pope John XXIII (1881-1963) addressed several prisoners in the Regina Coeli prison. After the Pope had spoken, a murderer was allowed to approach him, and asked, "Are those words of hope you have given us meant for such a great sinner as me?" The Pope embraced the murderer.[201]

Chapter 5: From Problem-Solving to Zen

Problem-Solving

• Boston Celtic Bill Russell's grandfather was a proud man who knew how to stick up for himself. Once, he worked a year for a white farmer, doing such things as plowing a field and planting seeds in return for a share of the sales of the crops. However, the white farmer did not pay him fairly when the crops were sold. Mr. Russell's grandfather let the white farmer know what he thought, and the white farmer threatened him. Mr. Russell's grandfather ended up pulling a gun on the white farmer, who threatened, "We'll get you for this! Tonight!" Mr. Russell's grandfather knew who would be coming that night: the Night Riders, aka the Ku Klux Klan. He first moved his family to safety, then he returned to his house with a gun and a dog. That night, as expected, the Night Raiders came, and they ordered Mr. Russell's grandfather to come out of the house and take a beating. He told them that they would have to come in the house after him. One of the Klansman fired a shot at the house, and Mr. Russell's grandfather fired his shotgun into the darkness. The Night Riders ran away.[202]

• Esther Nichols Wilbur, a Quaker, was fervently anti-slavery, and her house was a station on the Underground Railroad. One day, the local meetinghouse was to be the site of an anti-slavery meeting in the afternoon, but the caretaker was pro-slavery, and he decided to lock the abolitionists out of the meetinghouse after the Quaker worship in the morning. However, following morning worship, Ms. Wilbur remained seated, and she refused to leave despite the threats of the caretaker. Instead, she told him, "I am not preventing thee from locking the doors if thee wants to. I expect to stay for the afternoon meeting." The caretaker locked the doors and left her, and when it was time for the anti-slavery afternoon meeting, Ms. Wilbur simply unlocked the doors and let everybody else in.[203]

• As preachers' children, Cecil and Hugh Porter had to be polite to all of their neighbors, even the ones they didn't like. One day their father, Rev. Edwin Porter, who preached in Texas during the first half of the 20th century, discovered that Cecil and Hugh hadn't ever invited the Smith girls, Lucy and Jenny, to play tennis with them. Therefore, he gave his sons an ultimatum: Either invite the Smith girls to play tennis, or don't play tennis at all. Cecil and Hugh disliked the Smith girls, but they found a way out of their dilemma. They invited the Smith girls to play tennis in the afternoon of a sweltering Texas summer day. After a few games, the Smith girls decided that they didn't want to play tennis ever again and so regretfully declined all future invitations.[204]

• Tsukahara Bokuden founded a school of martial arts known as the Way of Winning Without Trying. In the practice of this martial art, the adept wins by figuring out how not to lose. One day Bokuden was traveling in a small boat with a few other people when a warrior on the boat challenged him to a duel. Bokuden suggested that they duel on a near-by small island. When they reached the island, the warrior stepped off the boat, walked onto the island, and unsheathed his sword. However, Bokuden, still standing in the boat, used a pole to shove the boat off the island and into the water, leaving the warrior stranded on the island.[205]

• In the 1850s, several students at Earlham College requested permission to go to the circus, but the Governor of the college said that they could go only as far as the front gate of the campus; therefore, the students removed the front gate and carried it in front of them as they walked to the circus. Once there, they explained the situation to the circus ticket man, who ordered a flap of the tent lifted up so they could bring the front gate inside the tent with them. After seeing the circus, they returned back to the campus and hung the gate where it belonged.[206]

• Taking care of Alzheimer's patients can be difficult. One Alzheimer's patient stood near an elevator, far from the place she was supposed to be. Her caretaker asked why she was there, and she replied, "I'm waiting for the bus." Her caretaker tried without success to get her to return to the place where she was supposed to be, but she resisted. Finally, the caretaker said, "I think the bus company is on strike." Only then did the Alzheimer's patient return to where she was supposed to be.[207]

• For many years, golf courses were sexist. At Sandwich, England, the Royal St. George's golf club did not allow women to become members; in fact, it did not even recognize the existence of women. However, it ran into a "problem" one year when Fiona MacDonald became a member of the Cambridge University golf team, which plays Royal St. George's each year. After taking thought, the members of Royal St. George's decided to make Ms. MacDonald an honorary man for the duration of the match.[208]

• Even as a child in Vermont, downhill mountain bike racer Missy Glover was resourceful. Often, she went on long bike rides with neighborhood boys. One evening, a snowstorm blew up suddenly and she and the boys didn't come home all night. Their parents were frantic, but the next day the children returned home. The boys were shaken, but young Missy was calm and collected as she explained what she had done in the emergency: "I built a shelter and we sat it out — it was incredible."[209]

• In the days when American schools were being desegregated, a black schoolchild had a problem. He had to walk two miles to go to a white school, but when he arrived, the white teacher wouldn't let him into the classroom because his shoes were dirty! The schoolchild's mother took away the teacher's excuse for banning her son from class by giving her son a bottle of shoe polish to carry with him so that he could polish his shoes before entering the school.[210]

• Early in his career, James W. Morrissey worked as a treasurer for railroad baron James Fisk, Jr. Late one night, he was summoned to see Mr. Fisk at the theater, and he had to step over approximately 50 burly men to see him. He later learned that the 50 burly men were present to make sure that no process-servers or deputy sheriffs were able to serve Mr. Fisk with papers requiring him to appear in court to answer questions concerning the Erie Railroad.[211]

• Mulla Nasrudin once walked by a lake into which a miser had fallen. Although some people were reaching for the miser and yelling, "Give me your hand," the miser kept treading water and shouting for help. Fortunately, Nasrudin quickly rescued the miser. When the other people asked how he had done it, he replied, "I knew that this miser refuses to give anything to anybody, so instead of saying 'Give me your hand,' I told him, 'Take my hand.'"[212]

• Jockey Julie Krone was four-foot-eleven and weighed 100 pounds, and she worried that horse trainers would think that she wasn't strong enough to handle their horses. To solve that problem, she developed a very strong handshake. One horse trainer remembered, "This cute little girl ... comes up to me and squeaks, 'Hi! I'm Julie Krone! I'm a jockey!' and takes my hand and *brings me to my knees.* Well, we let her ride, and she rides like a god."[213]

• A dervish possessed no other clothing than a ragged pair of pants. Seeing a rich man, he asked, "If I were to die today, what would you do for me?" The rich man replied, "I would have your body wrapped in a shroud, and then I would have your body buried." The dervish said, "Let me have a shirt now, while I can use it. When I die, let my body be buried naked."[214]

• Tip O'Neill drove his kids out of town to buy a puppy: a beagle they named Pokey. A problem arose on the way home: Which of the kids would be the one who would sit by the new puppy? Mr. O'Neill solved the problem by stopping the car every 15 minutes so the children could change seats and everybody would have a turn sitting by Pokey.[215]

• Immediately after beginning his pontificate, Pope John XXIII sometimes would wake up in the middle of the night, worrying about some problem, and decide that he would talk about it with the Pope, only to remember that he was the Pope. Whenever that happened, he would say to himself, "In that case, I'll talk it over with Our Lord!"[216]

• When race car driver Janet Guthrie was 16 years old, she wanted to take up parachute jumping. Her parents weren't sure that she should do that, so she demonstrated that she could handle the landing roll by jumping off the roof of their one-house story. This convinced her parents to allow her to learn to parachute jump.[217]

• During her close-ups in movies, Marlene Dietrich wanted her mouth muscles to be taut, so before each close-up shot, she sucked on lemons.[218]

Rabbis

• A case appeared before the Noda B'Yehudah in which an elegantly dressed man and a roughly dressed man pleaded. The roughly dressed man claimed that he was a rich man traveling far from home and friends and that the elegantly dressed man was his wagon driver, but that his wagon driver had robbed him and exchanged clothes with him. The elegantly dressed man denied ever having been a wagon driver. The Noda B'Yehudah said that he would think about the case, and then he would give them his judgment the next morning. The next morning, the two men arrived at the Noda B'Yehudah's house and sat outside as they waited for him, but they were ignored as the Noda B'Yehudah went about his business. Suddenly, the Noda B'Yehudah opened his door and ordered, "Wagon driver, come here!" The elegantly dressed man immediately stood up.[219]

• R' Meir Leibush, the Malbim, became the rabbi of Bucharest. The first Sabbath he was rabbi, he took a walk and observed many Jewish businesses open and conducting business. He then told the leaders of the community that he must resign, because he was afraid that he would not be paid. When the leaders asked how he could think such a thing, he replied, "When you appointed me rabbi of the city, you offered me a fine salary. I therefore said to myself: This is obviously a well-off community, which can afford to pay such a salary. Now I see that your people are so poor that they cannot survive by working only six days a week and are forced to work even on Shabbos, so how can you possibly have the money to pay me?"[220]

• Rabbi Shlomo Carlebach once led a tall man with long, stringy white hair, blue eyes, and an offensive odor to a place at a shul (synagogue) dinner, where the man devoured plate after plate of food. The man was a Christian from Texas who was obviously very hungry. Rabbi Shlomo had seen the man sitting on a bench in Central Park, and he had asked, "Do you need a meal?" The Christian said later, "I really don't know what I would have done if your Rabbi hadn't come by. I'll tell you honestly, this is the first meal I've eaten in three days. When he walked right up to me and asked, 'Brother, do you need a meal?,' I said to myself, this here man is surely an angel from God."[221]

• One Friday a group of traveling Jews arrived in a town and began looking for shelter, but none of the townspeople offered them hospitality. Therefore, the Jews sought the town's rabbi and explained their predicament. The rabbi quickly put on his Sabbath garments and told the traveling Jews to walk with him to the next town, where they would surely find hospitality. When the townspeople saw the rabbi walking out of town, they asked him why he was leaving. The rabbi explained, "Travelers aren't welcomed here, so I won't live in this town." The townspeople then offered hospitality to the travelers.[222]

Religion

• The Roman Empress lost a valuable bracelet just when Rabbi Samuel ben Sosratai visited Rome. The Empress caused a proclamation to be made, saying that if the bracelet was found and returned within 30 days, the person returning the bracelet would receive a reward, but if the bracelet was not returned within 30 days, anyone found possessing the bracelet would be put to death. Rabbi Samuel found the bracelet, but he deliberately waited 31 days before returning it to the Empress. She asked why he had deliberately waited until after the deadline to return the bracelet, and he answered, "So that you should not say that I returned it because I was afraid of you. I returned it because I fear God." The Empress then said, "Praised be the God of the Jews!"[223]

• During the Jewish holiday of Sukkos, Jews eat in a Sukkah — an outdoor shelter — to remind them of the shelters that their ancestors lived in after fleeing from captivity in Egypt. The shelters are set up only temporarily, then taken down after a few days. Once a government official passing through a town saw the shelters the Jews had set up to celebrate Sukkos and ordered the mayor of the town to have the shelters torn down as they had been built without government permission. Fortunately, the mayor was a friend of the Jews, and so he issued a proclamation that ordered the Jews to tear down the shelters within 10 days — plenty of time to celebrate Sukkos.[224]

• Around the year 1884, Sam W. Moreland attended a revival in the American frontier. During the preacher's sermon, some men arrived and said that the Indians had been raiding the land and had gotten all of Mr. Moreland's horses. Mr. Moreland said that he couldn't believe that, because before riding off to attend the revival, he had prayed to God to take care of his affairs. Still, Mr. Moreland rode off to see about his horses. Later, he rode back to the revival. The preacher knew that everyone was curious about the horses, so he allowed Mr. Moreland to make his report: "Not a horse gone." Then the sermon continued.[225]

• The maggid (traveling preacher) of Zlotchov was once asked how Abraham had kept all of God's laws since they had not yet been given to the World. The maggid replied that Abraham had asked himself before performing an action whether it would increase or decrease his love for God. If it would increase his love, then he knew that the action was the right thing to do.[226]

• New pastors should realize that their job is to speak and the job of the congregation is to listen. Furthermore, if the congregation ever finishes its job before the pastor's job is done, the pastor should catch up as quickly as possible.[227]

Signs

• A farmer wanted to protect his chickens from thieves, so he posted this sign by his chicken coop: "Anyone who loafs around my chicken house at night will be found still there the next morning."[228]

• After tennis champion Martina Navratilova defected from Czechoslovakia to the United States, she acquired the vanity license plate "X-CZECH."[229]

• Sign on a high school teacher's bulletin board: "FREE. Every Monday through Friday. Knowledge. Bring your own containers."[230]

Training and Trainers

• As a world-class women's gymnastics coach, Bela Karolyi emphasizes hard work. Before the 1996 Olympic Games were held in Atlanta, Mr. Karolyi was training a couple of U.S. team members at his ranch in Texas. A storm knocked out all the electricity to his ranch and gymnasium, but he simply opened the doors to the gym and held practice anyway.[231]

• Lucia Rijker is a European boxing champion whose nickname is "Lady Ali." After winning a boxing match against a tough opponent, she ran over to her trainer and tried to jump into his arms, but he was a new trainer, and he was much smaller than her old trainer. So, to celebrate her victory, she picked him up and lifted him over her head.[232]

• Some gymnasts do odd exercises. In the late 1970s, to build up the strength in their legs, some of coach Muriel Grossfeld's young girl gymnasts used to push cars up a slightly slanted driveway. Sometimes, drivers would see them and stop, thinking that the gymnasts needed help because their car was stalled.[233]

Travel

• In the summer of 1987, 16-year-old future soccer superstar Julie Foudy made some major moves in her favorite sport. She had been playing soccer well as a member of a local district team, and she was picked to play on a team that represented California. Within a month, she had played so well that she was picked to play on the West Regional team that competed in west Washington state. She played well there and was one of 18 girls picked to go to Michigan to play, so she called home to ask, "Mom, can you send more money? I don't know what's going on, but I have to go to Michigan." Once again, she played well, and she was picked to go to Blaine, Minnesota, to play on the national 19-and-under team. As you may expect by now, Julie played well and was chosen to play on yet another team. She called home again: "Mom! I need more money! I'm going to China! With the U.S. women's national team! They just put me on the team!" (In 1996, she won an Olympic gold medal as part of the United States national women's soccer team.)[234]

• When Julia Chang was a teenager, her relatives smuggled her out of mainland China so she could escape Communism. She took very little of value with her — except a coat with a lining to which $100 was pinned. In the United States, she attended Smith College in Northampton, Massachusetts, married Henry Lin, became an English professor at Ohio University in Athens, Ohio, and gave birth to Maya Lin, who is named after the Hindu goddess who is the mother of Buddha. Her middle name — Ying — is Chinese and means "precious stone." Like other teenagers, Maya Lin worked at McDonald's to earn spending money. Later, as an architecture student at Yale University, she designed the Vietnam Veterans Memorial on the Mall in Washington, D.C.[235]

• One day, Samson Raphael Hirsch, the leader of German Orthodoxy in the 19th century, decided to travel to Switzerland. This surprised his disciples, so he explained, "When I stand shortly before the Almighty, I will be held answerable to many questions, but what will I say when, and I am sure to be asked, 'Did you see my Alps?'"[236]

• A new museum was being built right on the rim of the Grand Canyon, one of the most majestic sights in the world. A bus dropped off several tourists — who ignored the Grand Canyon and instead watched the cement mixer.[237]

War

• Howard M. Jenkins, a Quaker, was totally opposed to war. After Mr. Jenkins had become editor of a Quaker newspaper, the *Friends Intelligencer*, a friend told him, "Thee is getting on well, Howard, except that almost all of thy editorials are about peace." Mr. Jenkins replied, "As long as civilized nations believe in war, I expect to give about 50 editorials a year to the subject. That will leave two weeks for other concerns."[238]

• In Czarist Russia, a company of Russians prepared to go into combat. The commandant told his soldiers, "Get your bayonets ready and prepare to meet your man in hand-to-hand combat." The lone Jew in his company raised his hand and asked, "Could you show me my man? Maybe we can come to an agreement."[239]

• A World War I soldier went to Paris, experienced part of the city, then said, "I wish I was seeing Paris before I became a Christian."[240]

Weight

• Pope John XXIII was a very stout man. Once, he saw a very stout carpenter working in the Vatican carpenter shop, so he told him, "I see that you belong to the same party that I do." When the carpenter protested that he didn't belong to any party, the Pope answered, "Yes, you become a member automatically — it's the Fat Man's Party."[241]

• As Pope John XXIII was walking in Rome, he heard a woman exclaim about how fat he was. Turning to the woman, he said, "But Madame, you must know that the conclave [meeting held to elect a Pope] is not exactly a beauty contest."[242]

Work

• Tom Danehy, columnist for the *Tucson Weekly*, ran a basketball tournament in the summer of 2009. He had hired a young woman who was a player on the Pima Community College team to operate the scoreboard. Tom says, "It's odd but true that the refs can make one or two (or 50) bad calls, and the players and crowd will do a little low-level grumbling. But if the score is wrong, or the clock isn't being stopped and/or started at the right times, they go nuts. I pointed this out to the young lady before we got started." Unfortunately, she kept texting throughout the games, although he kept telling her not to do that. Before the final game of the day, he gave her a choice. She could keep the $8.50 per hour that was her salary, or he could make the salary $15 per hour but subtract $1 for each time he saw her texting. She said that she would keep the $8.50 per hour. Afterward, she asked if she could work as a scorekeeper the following week. Mr. Danehy says, "I asked her if she would have her cell phone with her, and told her that my answer to her question would be the opposite of her answer to my question."[243]

• In September of 1900 Malcolm Glenn Wyer started a long career as a librarian when he began work at the University of Minnesota as the graduate reference assistant. Being intelligent and industrious, he made a number of suggestions for the improvement of the library, but was told by Dr. W.W. Folwell, his boss, "Probably you are right, but, you know, we must humor Miss L [his assistant] — for we think that she is losing her mind." By the way, while Mr. Wyer was working as a librarian at the State University of Iowa, the library was moved into temporary quarters. One day, Mr. Wyer showed the library to a group of college presidents, but explained to them that these were only temporary quarters. The President of the University of Minnesota, Dr. George E. Vincent, heard him and laughed, then explained, "My. Wyer, when you have been around universities as long as I have, you will find out that in a university nothing is more permanent than temporary quarters." Dr. Vincent was right — the library stayed in its "temporary" quarters for more than 45 years.[244]

• Actress Jennifer Lopez worked hard to get the title role in the career-making movie *Selena*. She studied the singer, copied her mannerisms, and even moved in with Selena's sister for a while. She also made a major impression on the movie producers during an 11-hour audition in which she sang two songs in the character of Selena and acted in five scenes. The hard work paid off. She won the role, and its success helped her become Hollywood's highest-paid Latina actress.[245]

• Among his other occupations, Nasrudin was a judge. While listening to the beginning of a complicated case, he told the plaintiff, "I think that you are right." Later, after hearing the defendant, Nasrudin told him, "I think that you are right." When the clerk of the court asked him, "How can both the plaintiff and the defendant be right? One of them must be wrong," Nasrudin replied, "I think that you are also right."[246]

• As a teenager, Julie Krone went to the Tampa Bay Downs in Florida to become a jockey. She met a trainer, Jerry Pace, who said to her, "I'm told you want to be a jockey." Mr. Krone replied, "No, I'm *going* to be a jockey." She did, and in 1993, she won the Belmont Stakes to become the first woman to win a Triple Crown race.[247]

• According to legend, Clark Gable and William Faulkner met in Hollywood. Mr. Gable asked, "What do you do, Mr. Faulkner?" Mr. Faulkner replied, "I write. And what do *you* do, Mr. Gable?"[248]

Zen

• Two monks were out walking, when they came to a river that they needed to cross. On the bank of the river was a woman who also needed to cross the river, so one of the monks offered to carry her, an act of kindness to which she agreed. The monks and the woman crossed the river, then the woman went in one direction and the monks in another. Long afterward, one of the monks told the monk who had carried the woman, "We have taken a vow to stay away from women. Why did you carry the woman across the river?" The other monk replied, "I set the woman down a long time ago. Why are you still carrying her?"[249]

• Zen master Rinzai once told an assembly of monks, "I spent 20 years with Obaku. When three times I asked him about the cardinal principle of Buddhism, he gave me three blows with his stick. It was like being patted with a branch of mugwort. I'd love another taste of that stick now. Who can give it to me?" A monk said, "I can." Rinzai then held out his stick toward the monk, but when the monk tried to take it from him, Rinzai used the stick to hit him.[250]

Appendix A: Bibliography

Aaseng, Nathan. *True Champions: Great Athletes and Their Off-the-Field Heroics.* New York: Walker and Company, 1993.

Adams, Joey. *The God Bit.* Boston, MA: G.K. Hall & Co., 1975.

Alley, Ken. *Awkward Christian Soldiers.* Wheaton, IL: Harold Shaw Publishers, 1998.

Aurand, Jr., A. Monroe. *Wit and Humor of the Pennsylvania Germans.* Harrisburg, PA: The Author, 1946.

Balcavage, Dynise. *Gabrielle Reece.* Philadelphia. PA: Chelsea House Publishers, 2001.

Banker, Stan. *Walk Cheerfully the Middleroad.* Richmond, IN: Friends United Press, 1994.

Berman, Connie. *Anna Kournikova.* Philadelphia. PA: Chelsea House Publishers, 2001.

Besserman, Perle and Manfred Steger. *Crazy Clouds: Zen Radicals, Rebels, and Reformers.* Boston, MA: Shambala, 1991.

Blackman, Sushila, compiler and editor. *Graceful Exits: How Great Beings Die.* New York: Weatherhill, Inc., 1997.

Buber, Martin, collector and editor. *Ten Rungs: Hasidic Sayings.* New York: Schocken Books, 1947.

Burchard, S.H. *Dorothy Hamill.* New York: Harcourt Brace Jovanovich, 1978.

Burton, Hal, editor. *Acting in the Sixties.* London: British Broadcasting Corporation, 1970.

Cantwell, Lois, and Pohla Smith. *Women Winners: Then and Now.* New York: Sports Illustrated for Kids, 2000.

Charles, Helen White, collector and editor. *Quaker Chuckles and Other True Stories About Friends.* Oxford, OH: H.W. Charles, 1961.

Chung, Tsai Chih (editor and illustrator) and Kok Kok Kiang (translator). *The Book of Zen.* Singapore: Asiapac, 1990.

Cleary, Thomas, translator. *Zen Antics: A Hundred Stories of Enlightenment.* Boston, MA: Shambhala Publications, Inc., 1993.

Clower, Jerry. *Ain't God Good!* Waco, TX: Word Books, Publisher, 1975.

Collins, Beulah, collector. *For Benefit of Clergy.* New York: Grosset & Dunlap, 1966.

Deedy, John. *A Book of Catholic Anecdotes.* Allen, TX: Thomas More, 1997.

Doonan, Simon. *Wacky Chicks: Life Lessons from Fearlessly Inappropriate and Fabulously Eccentric Women.* New York: Simon & Schuster, 2003.

Downing, Charles. *Tales of the Hodja*. New York: Henry Z. Walck, Inc., 1965.

Duncan, Kenn. *Divas: The Fabulous Photography of Kenn Duncan*. New York: Universe Publishing, 2008. Text by Stephen M. Silverman.

Epstein, Lawrence J. *A Treasury of Jewish Anecdotes*. Northvale, NJ: Jason Aronson, Inc., 1989.

Erskine, Carl. *Carl Erskine's Tales from the Dodger Dugout*. Champaigne, IL: Sports Publishing, Inc., 2000.

Fadiman, James and Robert Frager. *Essential Sufism*. San Francisco, CA: HarperSanFrancisco, 1997.

Farzan, Massud. *Another Way of Laughter: A Collection of Sufi Humor*. New York: E.P. Dutton & Co., Inc., 1973.

Fesquet, Henri, collector. *Wit and Wisdom of Good Pope John*. Translated by Salvator Attanasio. New York: P.J. Kenedy & Sons, 1964.

Fox, Patty. *Star Style: Hollywood Legends as Fashion Icons*. Santa Monica, CA: Angel City Press, Inc., 1995.

Frary, I.T. *At Large in Marble Halls*. Philadelphia, PA: Dorrance & Company, 1959.

Fricke, Aaron. *Reflections of a Rock Lobster: A Story About Growing Up Gay*. Boston, MA: AlyCat Books, 1981.

Frist, Karyn McLaughlin, editor. *"Love you, Daddy Boy": Daughters Honor the Fathers They Love*. Lanham, MD: Taylor Trade Publishing, 2006.

Furman, Leah. *Jennifer Lopez*. Philadelphia, PA: Chelsea House Publishers, 2001.

Galt, Margot Fortunato. *Up to the Plate: The All American Girls Professional Baseball League*. Minneapolis, MN: Lerner Publications Company, 1995.

Garvey, Reverend Francis J. *Favorite Humor of Famous Americans*. Kandiyohi, MN: Reverend Francis J. Garvey, 1981.

Gerler, William R. *Educator's Treasury of Humor for All Occasions*. West Nyack, NY: Parker Publishing Company, 1972.

Gershick, Zsa Zsa. *Gay Old Girls*. Los Angeles, CA: Alyson Books, 1998.

Goldenstern, Joyce. *American Women Against Violence*. Springfield, NJ: Enslow Publications, Inc., 1998.

Goodman, Philip. *Rejoice in Thy Festival*. New York: Bloch Publishing Company, 1956.

Greenberg, Jan, and Sandra Jordan. *Runaway Girl: The Artist Louise Bourgeois*. New York: Harry N. Abrams, Inc., 2003.

Grenfell, Joyce, et. al. *Joyce: By Herself and Her Friends*. London: Macdonald Futura Publishers, Limited, 1981.

Gross, David C., and Esther R. Gross, compilers. *Jewish Wisdom*. New York: Walker and Company, 1992.

Hadleigh, Boze. *Hollywood Gays*. New York: Barricade Books, Inc., 1996.

Hajdusiewicz, Babs Bell. *Mary Carter Smith: African-American Storyteller*. Springfield, NJ: Enslow Publications, Inc., 1995.

Hall, Marilyn, and Rabbi Jerome Cutler. *The Celebrity Kosher Cookbook*. Los Angeles, CA: J.P. Tarcher, Inc., 1975.

Haney, Lynn. *The Lady is a Jock*. New York: Dodd, Mead, and Company, 1973.

Haney, Lynn. *Perfect Balance: The Story of an Elite Gymnast*. New York: G.P. Putnam's Sons, 1979.

Harris, Nick. *I Wish I'd Said That!* London: Octopus Books, Limited, 1984.

Hay, Peter. *Movie Anecdotes*. New York: Oxford University Press, 1990.

Hecht, Andrew. *Hollywood Merry-Go-Round*. New York: Grosset and Dunlap, Publishers, 1947.

Hill, L.A. *Elementary Anecdotes in American English*. New York: Oxford University Press, 1980.

Himelstein, Shmuel. *A Touch of Wisdom, A Touch of Wit*. Brooklyn, NY: Mesorah Publications, Limited, 1991.

Himelstein, Shmuel. *Words of Wisdom, Words of Wit*. Brooklyn, NY: Mesorah Publications, Ltd., 1993.

Holcomb, Roy K., Samuel K. Holcomb, and Thomas K. Holcomb. *Deaf Culture Our Way: Anecdotes From the Deaf Community*. San Diego, CA: DawnSignPress, 1994.

Hollingsworth, Amy. *The Simple Faith of Mister Rogers*. Nashville, TN: Integrity Publishers, 2005.

Holloway, Gary. *Saints, Demons, and Asses: Southern Preacher Anecdotes*. Bloomington, IN: Indiana University Press, 1989.

Jacobs, J. Vernon, compiler. *450 True Stories from Church History*. Grand Rapids, MI: Wm. B. Eerdmans Publishing Company, 1955.

Jimenez, Laura. *Hear Me OUT!: A Dose of Lesbian Humor for the Whole Human Race*. San Jose, New York, Lincoln, Shanghai: Writers Club Press, 2001.

Jones, Betty Millsaps. *Wonder Women of Sports*. New York: Random House, 1981.

Karsh, Yousuf. *Canadians*. Toronto: University of Toronto Press, 1978.

Keller, Emily. *Margaret Bourke-White: A Photographer's Life*. Minneapolis, MN: Lerner Publications Company, 1996.

Klinger, Kurt, collector. *A Pope Laughs: Stories of John XXIII*. Translated by Sally McDevitt Cunneen. New York: Holt, Rinehart and Winston, 1964.

Knudson, R.R. *Martina Navratilova: Tennis Power*. New York: Viking Kestrel, 1986.

Kornfield, Jack, and Christina Feldman. *Soul Food: Stories to Nourish the Spirit and the Heart*. San Francisco, CA: HarperSanFrancisco, 1996. This is a revised edition of their 1991 book *Stories of the Spirit, Stories of the Heart*.

Leipold, L. Edmond. *Famous American Artists*. Minneapolis, MN: T.S. Denison and Company, Inc., 1969.

Lessa, Christina. *Gymnastics Balancing Acts*. New York: Universe Publishing, 1997.

Lessa, Christina. *Women Who Win: Stories of Triumph in Sport and in Life*. New York: Universe Publishing, 1998.

Lidz, Franz. *Unstrung Heroes: My Improbable Life with Four Impossible Uncles*. New York: Random House, 1991.

Lindop, Laurie. *Athletes*. New York: Twenty-First Century Books, 1996.

Linkletter, Art. *Kids Say the Darndest Things!* New York: Bonanza Books, 1978.

Linkletter, Art. *Oops! Or, Life's Awful Moments*. Garden City, NY: Doubleday & Company, Inc., 1967.

Lurie, Jon. *Allison's Story*. Minneapolis, MN: Lerner Publications Company, 1996.

Mabery, D.L. *George Lucas*. Minneapolis, MN: Lerner Publications Company, 1987.

Macht, Norman L. *Christy Mathewson*. New York: Chelsea House Publishers, 1991.

Malone, Mary. *Maya Lin: Architect and Artist*. Berkeley Heights, NJ: Enslow Publications, Inc., 1995.

Malone, Mary. *Will Rogers: Cowboy Philosopher*. Springfield, NJ: Enslow Publications, Inc., 1996.

Mandelbaum, Yitta Halberstam. *Holy Brother: Inspiring Stories and Enchanted Tales About Rabbi Shlomo Carlebach*. Northvale, NJ: Jason Aronson, Inc., 1997.

Marx, Groucho. *Groucho and Me*. New York: Bernard Geis Associates, 1959.

Masin, Herman L. *The Funniest Moments in Sports*. New York: M. Evans and Company, 1974.

McPhaul, John J. *Deadlines and Monkeyshines: The Fabled World of Chicago Journalism*. Englewood Cliffs, NJ: Prentice-Hall, Inc. 1962.

Mendelsohn, S. Felix. *Here's a Good One: Stories of Jewish Wit and Wisdom*. New York: Block Publishing Co., 1947.

Michaels, Louis. *The Humor and Warmth of Pope John XXIII: His Anecdotes and Legends*. New York: Pocket Books, Inc., 1965.

Midler, Bette. *A View from a Broad*. New York: Simon and Schuster, Inc., 1980.

Miller, Shannon. *Winning Every Day: Gold Medal Advice for a Happy, Healthy Life!* New York: Bantam Books, 1998.

Mindess, Harvey. *The Chosen People? A Testament, Both Old and New, to the Therapeutic Power of Jewish Wit and Humor*. Los Angeles, CA: Nash Publishing Corporation, 1972.

Molen, Sam. *Take 2 and Hit to Right*. Philadelphia, PA: Dorrance and Company, 1959.

Moore, Michael. *Stupid White Men*. New York: HarperCollins Publishers, Inc., 2001.

Morrissey, James W. *Noted Men and Women*. New York: The Klebold Press, 1910.

Moskowitz-Mateu, Lysa, and David LaFontaine. *Poison Pen: The True Confessions of Two Tabloid Reporters*. Los Angeles, CA: Dove Books, 1996.

Muallimoglu, Nejat. *The Wit and Wisdom of Nasraddin Hodja*. New York: Cynthia Parzych Publishing, Inc., 1986.

Mullen, Tom. *Living Longer and Other Sobering Possibilities*. Richmond, IN: Friends United Press, 1996.

Mullen, Tom. *Seriously, Life is a Laughing Matter*. Waco, TX: Word Books, 1978.

Neff, Fred. *Lessons from the Japanese Masters*. Minneapolis, MN: Lerner Publications Company, 1995.

Nirgiotis, Nicholas, and Theodore Nirgiotis. *No More Dodos: How Zoos Help Endangered Wildlife*. Minneapolis, MN: Lerner Publications Company, 1996.

Perry, Joel. *Funny That Way: Adventures in Fabulousness*. Los Angeles, CA: Alyson Books, 2001.

Petuchowski, Jakob J., translator and editor. *Our Masters Taught: Rabbinic Stories and Sayings*. New York: Crossroad, 1982.

Pflueger, Lynda. *Thomas Nast: Political Cartoonist*. Berkeley Heights, NJ: Enslow Publications, Inc., 2000.

Phares, Ross. *Bible in Pocket, Gun in Hand: The Story of Frontier Religion*. Garden City, NY: Doubleday & Company, Inc., 1964.

Porter, Alyene. *Papa was a Preacher*. New York: Abingdon Press, 1944.

Rabinowicz, Rabbi Dr. H. *A Guide to Hassidism*. New York: Thomas Yoseloff, 1960.

Rappoport, Ken, and Barry Wilner. *Girls Rule! The Glory and Spirit of Women in Sports*. Kansas City, MO: Andrews McMeel Publishing, 2000.

Riley, Gail Blasser. *Wah Ming Chang: Artist and Master of Special Effects*. Springfield, NJ: Enslow Publications, Inc., 1995.

Rowell, Edward K., editor. *Humor for Preaching and Teaching*. Grand Rapids, MI: Baker Books, 1996.

Russell, Bill. *Red and Me: My Coach, My Lifelong Friend*. With Alan Steinberg. New York: HarperCollins Publishers, 2009.

Rutledge, Rachel. *The Best of the Best in Gymnastics*. Brookfield, CT: The Millbrook Press, 1999.

Salzberg, Sharon. *A Heart as Wide as the World: Stories on the Path to Lovingkindness*. Boston, MA: Shambhala Publications, Inc., 1997.

Samra, Cal and Rose, editors. *Holy Hilarity*. Colorado Springs, CO: WaterBrook Press, 1999.

Samra, Cal and Rose, editors. *More Holy Hilarity*. Colorado Springs, CO: WaterBrook Press, 1999.

Savage, Jeff. *Julie Foudy: Soccer Superstar*. Minneapolis, MN: Lerner Publications Company, 1999.

Savage, Jeff. *Julie Krone: Unstoppable Jockey*. Minneapolis, MN: Lerner Publications Company, 1996.

Schafer, Kermit. *All Time Great Bloopers*. New York: Avenel Books, 1973.

Sessions, William H., collector. *More Quaker Laughter*. York, England: William Sessions, Limited, 1974.

Shah, Idries. *The Exploits of the Incomparable Mulla Nasrudin*. New York: E.P. Dutton and Co., 1966.

Shah, Idries. *The Pleasantries of the Incredible Mulla Nasrudin*. New York: E.P. Dutton and Co., 1968.

Silverman, William B. *Rabbinic Wisdom and Jewish Values*. New York: Union of American Hebrew Congregations, 1971.

Simons II, Minot. *Women's Gymnastics: A History. Volume 1: 1966 to 1974*. Carmel, CA: Welwyn Publishing Company, 1995.

Stafford, Nikki, editor. *Trekkers: True Stories by Fans for Fans*. Toronto, Ontario, Canada: ECW Press, 2002.

Stambler, Irwin. *Women in Sports*. Garden City, NY: Doubleday, 1975.

Steffens, Bradley, and Robyn M. Weaver. *Cartoonists*. San Diego, CA: Lucent Books, 2000.

Stefoff, Rebecca. *Mary Tyler Moore: The Woman Behind the Smile*. New York: New American Library, 1986.

Stewart, Whitney. *Sir Edmund Hillary: To Everest and Beyond*. Minneapolis, MN: Lerner Publications Company, 1996.

Strug, Kerri. *Landing on My Feet: A Diary of Dreams*. With John P. Lopez. Kansas City, MO: Andrews McMeel Publishing, 1997.

Tanner, Stephen. *Opera Antics and Anecdotes*. Toronto, Canada: Sound and Vision, 1999.

Telushkin, Rabbi Joseph. *Jewish Humor: What the Best Jewish Jokes Say About the Jews*. New York: William Morrow and Company, 1992.

Telushkin, Rabbi Joseph. *Jewish Wisdom: Ethical, Spiritual, and Historical Lessons from the Great Works and Thinkers*. New York: William Morrow and Company, Inc., 1994.

Tsai, Chih-Chung (editor and illustrator) and Kok Kok Kiang (translator). *The Book of Zen*. Singapore: Asiapac, 1990.

Tsai, Chih-Chung. *Zen Speaks: Shouts of Nothingness*. New York: Anchor Books, 1994.

Tsui, Cristy. *Women's Gymnastics Trivia*. Chicago, IL: Handstand Media, Inc., 2001.

Van Dyke, Dick. *Faith, Hope and Hilarity*. Edited by Ray Parker. Garden City, NY: Doubleday and Company, Inc, 1970.

Wade, Don. *"And Then Arnie Told Chi Chi ...."* Chicago, IL: Contemporary Books, 1993.

Wadsworth, Ginger. *Susan Butcher: Sled Dog Racer*. Minneapolis, MN: Lerner Publications Company, 1994.

Ward, Gene and Dick Hyman, collectors. *Football Wit and Humor*. New York: Grosset & Dunlap, Publishers, 1970.

Ward, Hiley H., editor. *Ecumania: The Humor That Happens When Catholics, Jews, and Protestants Come Together*. New York: Association Press, 1968.

Waters, John. *Crackpot: The Obsessions of John Waters*. New York: Vintage Books, 1987.

Wilner, Barry. *Michelle Kwan: Star Figure Skater*. Berkeley Heights, NJ: Enslow Publications, Inc., 2001.

Woughter, William. *All Preachers of Our God & King*. Wheaton, IL: Harold Shaw Publishers, 1997.

Wulffson, Don L. *Amazing True Stories*. New York: Cobblehill Books, 1991.

Wyer, Malcolm Glenn. *Books and People: Short Anecdotes from a Long Experience*. Denver, CO: The Old West Publishing Co., 1964.

Yamane, Linda. *Weaving a California Tradition: A Native American Basketmaker*. Minneapolis, MN: Lerner Publications Company, 1997.

Young, Alan, and Bill Burt. *Mr. Ed and Me*. New York: St. Martin's Press, 1994.

Zuckerman, Andrew. *Wisdom*. Edited by Alex Vlack. New York: Harry N. Abrams, Inc., 2008.

Appendix B: About the Author

It was a dark and stormy night. Suddenly a cry rang out, and on a hot summer night in 1954, Josephine, wife of Carl Bruce, gave birth to a boy — me. Unfortunately, this young married couple allowed Reuben Saturday, Josephine's brother, to name their first-born. Reuben, aka "The Joker," decided that Bruce was a nice name, so he decided to name me Bruce Bruce. I have gone by my middle name — David — ever since.

Being named Bruce David Bruce hasn't been all bad. Bank tellers remember me very quickly, so I don't often have to show an ID. It can be fun in charades, also. When I was a counselor as a teenager at Camp Echoing Hills in Warsaw, Ohio, a fellow counselor gave the signs for "sounds like" and "two words," then she pointed to a bruise on her leg twice. Bruise Bruise? Oh yeah, Bruce Bruce is the answer!

Uncle Reuben, by the way, gave me a haircut when I was in kindergarten. He cut my hair short and shaved a small bald spot on the back of my head. My mother wouldn't let me go to school until the bald spot grew out again.

Of all my brothers and sisters (six in all), I am the only transplant to Athens, Ohio. I was born in Newark, Ohio, and have lived all around Southeastern Ohio. However, I moved to Athens to go to Ohio University and have never left.

At Ohio U, I never could make up my mind whether to major in English or Philosophy, so I got a bachelor's degree with a double major in both areas, then I added a Master of Arts degree in English and a Master of Arts degree in Philosophy. Yes, I have my MAMA degree.

Currently, and for a long time to come (I eat fruits and veggies), I am spending my retirement writing books such as *Nadia Comaneci: Perfect 10*, *The Funniest People in Comedy*, *Homer's* Iliad: *A Retelling in Prose*, and *William Shakespeare's* Hamlet: *A Retelling in Prose*.

If all goes well, I will publish one or two books a year for the rest of my life. (On the other hand, a good way to make God laugh is to tell Her your plans.)

By the way, my sister Brenda Kennedy writes romances such as *A New Beginning* and *Shattered Dreams*.

Appendix C: Some Books by David Bruce

Anecdote Collections

250 Anecdotes About Opera
250 Anecdotes About Religion
250 Anecdotes About Religion: Volume 2
250 Music Anecdotes
Be a Work of Art: 250 Anecdotes and Stories
The Coolest People in Art: 250 Anecdotes
The Coolest People in the Arts: 250 Anecdotes
The Coolest People in Books: 250 Anecdotes
The Coolest People in Comedy: 250 Anecdotes
Create, Then Take a Break: 250 Anecdotes
Don't Fear the Reaper: 250 Anecdotes
The Funniest People in Art: 250 Anecdotes
The Funniest People in Books: 250 Anecdotes
The Funniest People in Books, Volume 2: 250 Anecdotes
The Funniest People in Books, Volume 3: 250 Anecdotes
The Funniest People in Comedy: 250 Anecdotes
The Funniest People in Dance: 250 Anecdotes
The Funniest People in Families: 250 Anecdotes
The Funniest People in Families, Volume 2: 250 Anecdotes
The Funniest People in Families, Volume 3: 250 Anecdotes
The Funniest People in Families, Volume 4: 250 Anecdotes
The Funniest People in Families, Volume 5: 250 Anecdotes
The Funniest People in Families, Volume 6: 250 Anecdotes
The Funniest People in Movies: 250 Anecdotes
The Funniest People in Music: 250 Anecdotes
The Funniest People in Music, Volume 2: 250 Anecdotes
The Funniest People in Music, Volume 3: 250 Anecdotes
The Funniest People in Neighborhoods: 250 Anecdotes
The Funniest People in Relationships: 250 Anecdotes
The Funniest People in Sports: 250 Anecdotes
The Funniest People in Sports, Volume 2: 250 Anecdotes
The Funniest People in Television and Radio: 250 Anecdotes
The Funniest People in Theater: 250 Anecdotes

The Funniest People Who Live Life: 250 Anecdotes
The Funniest People Who Live Life, Volume 2: 250 Anecdotes
The Kindest People Who Do Good Deeds, Volume 1: 250 Anecdotes
The Kindest People Who Do Good Deeds, Volume 2: 250 Anecdotes
Maximum Cool: 250 Anecdotes
The Most Interesting People in Movies: 250 Anecdotes
The Most Interesting People in Politics and History: 250 Anecdotes
The Most Interesting People in Politics and History, Volume 2: 250 Anecdotes
The Most Interesting People in Politics and History, Volume 3: 250 Anecdotes
The Most Interesting People in Religion: 250 Anecdotes
The Most Interesting People in Sports: 250 Anecdotes
The Most Interesting People Who Live Life: 250 Anecdotes
The Most Interesting People Who Live Life, Volume 2: 250 Anecdotes
Reality is Fabulous: 250 Anecdotes and Stories
Resist Psychic Death: 250 Anecdotes
Seize the Day: 250 Anecdotes and Stories

---

[1] Source: Hal Burton, editor, *Acting in the Sixties*, p. 211.

[2] Source: Kenn Duncan, *Divas: The Fabulous Photography of Kenn Duncan*, p. 42.

[3] Source: Peter Hay, *Movie Anecdotes*, p. 211.

[4] Source: S. Felix Mendelsohn, *Here's a Good One*, p. 236.

[5] Source: Charles Downing, *Tales of the Hodja*, pp. 26-27.

[6] Source: Rabbi Dr. H. Rabinowicz, *A Guide to Hassidism*, p. 121.

[7] Source: "20 Questions: Casey Driessen." Popmatters.com. 13 January 2009 <http://www.popmatters.com/pm/feature/68937-casey-driessen/>.

[8] Source: Nathan Aaseng, *True Champions: Great Athletes and Their Off-the-Field Heroics*, pp. 66, 75.

[9] Source: Stephen Tanner, *Opera Antics and Anecdotes*, pp. 128.

[10] Source: Ken Alley, *Awkward Christian Soldiers*, p. 18.

[11] Source: Nicholas Nirgiotis and Theodore Nirgiotis, *No More Dodos: How Zoos Help Endangered Wildlife*, pp. 27, 30.

[12] Source: Ginger Wadsworth, *Susan Butcher: Sled Dog Racer*, pp. 30, 44, 53.

[13] Source: Emily Keller, *Margaret Bourke-White: A Photographer's Life*, pp. 23, 94.

[14] Source: William H. Sessions, collector, *More Quaker Laughter*, p. 105.

[15] Source: Yousuf Karsh, *Canadians*, pp. 136-137.

[16] Source: Jan Greenberg and Sandra Jordan, *Runaway Girl: The Artist Louise Bourgeois*, p. 17.

[17] Source: Stephen Tanner, *Opera Antics and Anecdotes*, pp. 54-55.

[18] Source: Nick Harris, *I Wish I'd Said That!*, p. 28.

[19] Source: BartcopE. "Daily Page." 6 August 2009 <http://www.suprmchaos.com/home.index.html>.

[20] Source: Rachel Rutledge, *The Best of the Best in Gymnastics*, p. 41.

[21] Source: Carl Erskine, *Carl Erskine's Tales from the Dodger Dugout*, pp. 104-106.

[22] Source: Norman L. Macht, *Christy Mathewson*, pp. 16-17.

[23] Source: Carl Erskine, *Carl Erskine's Tales from the Dodger Dugout*, p. 98.

[24] Source: Joey Adams, *The God Bit*, pp. 261-262.

[25] Source: Betty Millsaps Jones, *Wonder Women of Sports*, pp. 43-46.

[26] Source: Sam Molen, *Take 2 and Hit to Right*, p. 20.

[27] Source: Malcolm Glenn Wyer, *Books and People*, p. 24.

[28] Source: Amy Hollingsworth, *The Simple Faith of Mister Rogers*, pp. 4-5.

[29] Source: Lynn Haney, *The Lady is a Jock*, p. 120.

[30] Source: David C. and Esther R. Gross, *Jewish Wisdom*, pp. 14-15.

[31] Source: Art Linkletter, *Kids Say the Darnest Things!*, p. 232.

[32] Source: Kurt Klinger, *A Pope Laughs*, p. 67.

[33] Source: Edward K. Rowell, editor, *Humor for Preaching and Teaching*, p. 37.

[34] Source: Leah Furman, *Jennifer Lopez*, pp. 17-18.

[35] Source: Nejat Muallimoglu, *The Wit and Wisdom of Nasraddin Hodja*, p. 2.

[36] Source: Nikki Stafford, editor, *Trekkers: True Stories by Fans for Fans*, p. 23.

[37] Source: Don Wade, *"And Then Arnie Told Chi Chi...,"* p. 128.

[38] Source: James W. Morrissey, *Noted Men and Women*, p. 39.

[39] Source: Lynda Pflueger, *Thomas Nast: Political Cartoonist*, p. 30.

[40] Source: Dick Van Dyke, *Faith, Hope, and Hilarity*, p. 141.

[41] Source: R.R. Knudson, *Martina Navratilova: Tennis Power*, p. 15.

[42]Source: Jeff Savage, *Julie Krone: Unstoppable Jockey*, p. 16.

[43]Source: Barry Wilner, *Michelle Kwan: Star Figure Skater*, p. 18.

[44]Source: Lynda Pflueger, *Thomas Nast: Political Cartoonist*, p. 98.

[45]Source: Rachel Rutledge, *The Best of the Best in Gymnastics*, p. 51.

[46]Source: Cal and Rose Samra, *Holy Hilarity*, p. 181.

[47]Source: Nejat Muallimoglu, *The Wit and Wisdom of Nasraddin Hodja*, p. 46.

[48]Source: Margot Fortunato Galt, *Up to the Plate: The All American Girls Professional Baseball League*, pp. 19, 46.

[49] Source: Dynise Balcavage, *Gabrielle Reece*, pp. 9, 12.

[50]Source: Herman L. Masin, *The Funniest Moments in Sports*, p. 58.

[51]Source: Jack Kornfield and Christina Feldman, *Soul Food*, p. 23.

[52] Source: Brad Darrach, "Meryl Streep On Top — And Tough Enough To Stay There: Enchanting, Colorless, Glacial, Fearless, Sneaky, Seductive, Manipulative, Magical Meryl." *Life Magazine*. December 1987 <http://www.maryellenmark.com/text/magazines/life/905W-000-034.html>.

[53]Source: Chih Chung Tsai, *Zen Speaks,* p. 37.

[54]Source: Jerry Clower, *Ain't God Good!*, pp. 175-176.

[55] Source: Jakob J. Petuchowski, translator and editor, *Our Masters Taught*, p. 21.

[56] Source: John J. McPhaul, *Deadlines and Monkeyshines: The Fabled World of Chicago Journalism*, p. 131.

[57]Source: Sharon Salzberg, *A Heart as Wide as the World*, pp. 122-123.

[58]Source: Sushila Blackman, compiler and editor, *Graceful Exits*, p. 82.

[59] Source: Dynise Balcavage, *Gabrielle Reece*, p. 20.

[60]Source: Simon Doonan, *Wacky Chicks*, pp. 101-102.

[61]Source: Mary Malone, *Maya Lin: Architect and Artist*, pp. 26-27.

[62]Source: Perle Besserman and Manfred Steger, *Crazy Clouds*, p. 89.

[63]Source: Dick Van Dyke, *Faith, Hope, and Hilarity*, p. 79,

[64] Source: Bill Russell, *Red and Me: My Coach, My Lifelong Friend*, pp. 3-4.

[65]Source: Jon Lurie, *Allison's Story*, pp. 6, 8, 11-13.

[66]Source: Fred Neff, *Lessons from the Japanese Masters*, p. 6.

[67] Source: Rabbi Joseph Telushkin, *Jewish Humor*, pp. 170-171.

[68] Source: Jack Kornfield and Christina Feldman, *Soul Food*, pp. 252-253.

[69] Source: Jeff Savage, *Julie Foudy: Soccer Superstar*, p. 41.

[70] Source: Fred Neff, *Lessons from the Japanese Masters*, p. 14.

[71] Source: D.L. Mabery, *George Lucas*, pp. 6, 26.

[72] Source: Tsai Chih Chung (editor and illustrator) and Kok Kok Kiang (translator), *The Book of Zen*, p. 45.

[73] Source: Hal Burton, editor, *Acting in the Sixties*, pp. 237-238.

[74] Source: Yitta Halberstam Mandelbaum, *Holy Brother*, p. 9.

[75] Source: Connie Berman, *Anna Kournikova*, pp. 51-52.

[76] Source: Lawrence J. Epstein, *A Treasury of Jewish Anecdotes*, p. 83.

[77] Source: S. Felix Mendelsohn, *Here's a Good One*, p. 221.

[78] Source: Martin Buber, *Ten Rungs*, pp. 64-65.

[79] Source: Rabbi Joseph Telushkin, *Jewish Humor*, p. 46.

[80] Source: Chih-Chung Tsai (editor and illustrator) and Kok Kok Kiang (translator), *The Book of Zen*, p. 109.

[81] Source: Michael Moore, *Stupid White Men*, p. 116.

[82] Source: Rabbi Joseph Telushkin, *Jewish Wisdom*, p. 5.

[83] Source: Gene Ward and Dick Hyman, *Football Wit and Humor*, p. 201.

[84] Source: James Fadiman and Robert Frager, *Essential Sufism*, pp. 81-82.

[85] Source: Bradley Steffens and Robyn M. Weaver, *Cartoonists*, p. 89.

[86] Source: Sushila Blackman, compiler and editor, *Graceful Exits*, p. 73.

[87] Source: Michael Moore, *Stupid White Men*, p. 117.

[88] Source: Sam Molen, *Take 2 and Hit to Right*, p. 35.

[89] Source: Connie Berman, *Anna Kournikova*, pp. 41-42.

[90] Source: Nikki Stafford, editor, *Trekkers: True Stories by Fans for Fans*, p. 3.

[91] Source: Andrew Tobias, "Boozy Nine Year Olds Avoiding Estate Tax In West Branch Iowa." 14 April 2009 <http://www.andrewtobias.com/newcolumns/090414.html >.

[92] Source: Karyn McLaughlin Frist, editor, *"Love you, Daddy Boy": Daughters Honor the Fathers They Love*, p. 193.

[93]Source: Rebecca Stefoff, *Mary Tyler Moore: The Woman Behind the Smile*, p. 34.

[94]Source: Kermit Schafer, *All Time Great Bloopers*, p. 32.

[95] Source: Anthony Bourdain, "My war on fast food." *The Guardian*. 12 June 2010 <http://www.guardian.co.uk/lifeandstyle/2010/jun/12/anthony-bourdain-war-fast-food>. By the way, "poo" is British for "excrement."

[96]Source: Idries Shah, *The Exploits of the Incomparable Nasrudin*, p. 29.

[97]Source: D.L. Mabery, *George Lucas*, pp. 23, 35-36.

[98]Source: Sharon Salzberg, *A Heart as Wide as the World*, pp. 45-46.

[99]Source: Marilyn Hall and Rabbi Jerome Cutler, *The Celebrity Kosher Cookbook*, p. 44.

[100]Source: Margot Fortunato Galt, *Up to the Plate: The All American Girls Professional Baseball League*, pp. 58-59.

[101]Source: Massud Farzan, *Another Way of Laughter*, p. 43.

[102] Source: Meghan Daum, "A colorful death by tobacco." *Los Angeles Times*. 24 June 2010 <http://www.latimes.com/news/opinion/commentary/la-oe-daum-camellights-20100624,0,5601747.column>.

[103]Source: Charles Downing, *Tales of the Hodja*, p. 26.

[104] Source: Andrew Zuckerman, *Wisdom*, p. 148.

[105]Source: Whitney Stewart, *Sir Edmund Hillary: To Everest and Beyond*, pp. 67-68.

[106]Source: Laura Jimenez, *Hear Me OUT!: A Dose of Lesbian Humor for the Whole Human Race*, p. 89.

[107]Source: Jerry Clower, *Ain't God Good!*, p. 176.

[108]Source: Hiley H. Ward, editor, *Ecumania*, p. 43.

[109]Source: Aaron Fricke, *Reflections of a Rock Lobster: A Story About Growing Up Gay*, pp. 53, 105-106.

[110]Source: Zsa Zsa Gershick, *Gay Old Girls*, p. 220.

[111]Source: Lysa Moskowitz-Mateu and David LaFontaine, *Poison Pen*, p. 166.

[112]Source: Joel Perry, *Funny That Way: Adventures in Fabulousness*, p. 109.

[113]Source: Betty Millsaps Jones, *Wonder Women of Sports*, pp. 14-18.

[114]Source: Idries Shah, *The Exploits of the Incomparable Nasrudin*, p. 158.

[115] Source: Leo Hickman, "Ten things I can't live without." *The Guardian.* 29 July 2009 <http://www.guardian.co.uk/environment/2009/jul/29/10-essential-things>.

[116] Source: Yousuf Karsh, *Canadians*, pp. 168-169.

[117] Source: Alan Young, *Mr. Ed and Me*, p. 49.

[118] Source: Louis Michaels, *The Humor and Warmth of Pope John XXIII*, p. 73.

[119] Source: Linda Yamane, *Weaving a California Tradition: A Native American Basketmaker*, p. 9.

[120] Source: Mary Malone, *Will Rogers: Cowboy Philosopher*, p. 92.

[121] Source: Thomas Cleary, translator, *Zen Antics*, pp. 21-22.

[122] Source: Nathan Aaseng, *True Champions: Great Athletes and Their Off-the-Field Heroics*, pp. 89-92.

[123] Source: Art Linkletter, *Oops!*, p. 111.

[124] Source: Shmuel Himelstein, *A Touch of Wisdom, A Touch of Wit*, p. 250.

[125] Source: Kenn Duncan, *Divas: The Fabulous Photography of Kenn Duncan*, p. 198.

[126] Source: Rev. Francis J. Garvey, *Favorite Humor of Famous Americans*, pp. 21-22.

[127] Source: L. Edmond Leipold, *Famous American Artists*, p. 24.

[128] Source: Helen White Charles, collector and editor, *Quaker Chuckles*, p. 4.

[129] Source: William B. Silverman, *Rabbinic Wisdom and Jewish Values*, pp. 95-96.

[130] Source: Rabbi Dr. H. Rabinowicz, *A Guide to Hassidism*, p. 104.

[131] Source: Ken Alley, *Awkward Christian Soldiers*, p. 90.

[132] Source: J. Vernon Jacobs, compiler, *450 True Stories from Church History*, pp. 51-52.

[133] Source: Andrew Hecht, *Hollywood Merry-Go-Round*, p. 67.

[134] Source: Shmuel Himelstein, *Words of Wisdom, Words of Wit*, pp. 237-238.

[135] Source: Marilyn Hall and Rabbi Jerome Cutler, *The Celebrity Kosher Cookbook*, p. 51.

[136] Source: Tom Mullen, *Living Longer and Other Sobering Possibilities*, p. 8.

[137] Source: Ken Rappoport and Barry Wilner, *Girls Rule!*, pp. 113-115.

[138]Source: Lynn Haney, *The Lady is a Jock*, p. 49.

[139]Source: John Deedy, *A Book of Catholic Anecdotes*, p. 137

[140]Source: Kerri Strug, *Landing on My Feet*, p. 49.

[141]Source: L.A. Hill, *Elementary Anecdotes in American English*, p. 42.

[142]Source: Roy K. Holcomb, Samuel K. Holcomb, and Thomas K. Holcomb, *Deaf Culture Our Way*, pp. 6, 73.

[143]Source: Groucho Marx, *Groucho and Me*, p. 321.

[144]Source: Herman L. Masin, *The Funniest Moments in Sports*, p. 33.

[145]Source: Joyce Grenfell, et. al., *Joyce*, p. 157.

[146]Source: Alyene Porter, *Papa was a Preacher*, p. 38.

[147]Source: William H. Sessions, collector, *More Quaker Laughter*, p. 107.

[148]Source: Beulah Collins, collector, *For Benefit of Clergy*, pp. 74-75.

[149]Source: Cal and Rose Samra, *More Holy Hilarity*, p. 130.

[150]Source: Irwin Stambler, *Women in Sports*, pp. 22-23, 29-30.

[151]Source: Christina Lessa, *Gymnastics Balancing Acts*, p. 149.

[152] Source: John J. McPhaul, *Deadlines and Monkeyshines: The Fabled World of Chicago Journalism*, pp. 118-119.

[153]Source: Lysa Moskowitz-Mateu and David LaFontaine, *Poison Pen*, pp. 152, 191.

[154] Source: Roger Ebert, "The best damn job in the whole damn world." 3 April 2009 <http://blogs.suntimes.com/ebert/2009/04/the_best_job_in_the_world.html>.

[155]Source: Christina Lessa, *Women Who Win*, p. 59.

[156] Source: "20 Questions: Jim White." 31 March 2008 <http://www.popmatters.com/pm/features/article/56691/jim-white/>.

[157]Source: S.H. Burchard, *Dorothy Hamill*, pp. 34, 36, 48.

[158]Source: John Waters, *Crackpot: The Obsessions of John Waters*, p. 62.

[159]Source: Bette Midler, *A View from a Broad*, pp. 40, 65.

[160]Source: Gary Holloway, *Saints, Demons, and Asses*, pp. 47-48.

[161]Source: William Woughter, *All Preachers of Our God & King*, p. 82.

[162]Source: Joel Perry, *Funny That Way: Adventures in Fabulousness*, p. 103.

[163]Source: Patty Fox, *Star Style: Hollywood Legends as Fashion Icons*, p. 64.

[164] Source: Roger Ebert, "The best damn job in the whole damn world." 3 April 2009 <http://blogs.suntimes.com/ebert/2009/04/the_best_job_in_the_world.html>.

[165] Source: Don L. Wulffson, *Amazing True Stories*, p. 34.

[166] Source: Ginger Wadsworth, *Susan Butcher: Sled Dog Racer*, pp. 22, 31.

[167] Source: Chih-Chung Tsai (editor and illustrator) and Kok Kok Kiang (translator), *The Book of Zen*, p. 67.

[168] Source: Lawrence J. Epstein, *A Treasury of Jewish Anecdotes*, p. 93.

[169] Source: Laurie Lindop, *Athletes*, p. 49.

[170] Source: Yitta Halberstam Mandelbaum, *Holy Brother*, p. 65.

[171] Source: Lynn Haney, *Perfect Balance*, p. 35.

[172] Source: Harvey Mindess, *The Chosen People?*, p. 47.

[173] Source: Cristy Tsui, *Women's Gymnastics Trivia*, pp. 161-162.

[174] Source: Shannon Miller, *Winning Every Day*, p. 21.

[175] Source: Dave Itzkoff, "Steve Martin brings it all home with his banjo." *The Guardian*. 5 August 2009 <http://www.guardian.co.uk/music/2009/aug/05/steve-martin-banjo-dolly-parton>.

[176] Source: Will Harris, "A Chat with Cy Curnin." Bullz-eye.com. 4 January 2008 <http://www.bullz-eye.com/music/interviews/2008/cy_curnin.htm>.

[177] Source: Babs Bell Hajdusiewicz, *Mary Carter Smith: African-American Storyteller*, p. 35.

[178] Source: Norman L. Macht, *Christy Mathewson*, p. 33.

[179] Source: Rev. Francis J. Garvey, *Favorite Humor of Famous Americans*, pp. 16-17.

[180] Source: John Deedy, *A Book of Catholic Anecdotes*, pp. 91-92.

[181] Source: Lois Cantwell and Pohla Smith, *Women Winners: Then and Now*, p. 57.

[182] Source: Cristy Tsui, *Women's Gymnastics Trivia*, pp. 65-66.

[183] Source: Barry Wilner, *Michelle Kwan: Star Figure Skater*, p. 16.

[184] Source: Franz Lidz, *Unstrung Heroes*, "About the Author," at end.

[185] Source: Ken Rappoport and Barry Wilner, *Girls Rule!*, p. 90.

[186]Source: Minot Simons II, *Women's Gymnastics: A History. Volume 1: 1966 to 1974*, pp. 100, 370.

[187]Source: Roy K. Holcomb, Samuel K. Holcomb, and Thomas K. Holcomb, *Deaf Culture Our Way*, pp. 23-24.

[188]Source: Amy Hollingsworth, *The Simple Faith of Mister Rogers*, p. 114.

[189]Source: John Waters, *Crackpot: The Obsessions of John Waters*, pp. 60-61.

[190]Source: Gail Blasser Riley, *Wah Ming Chang: Artist and Master of Special Effects*, pp. 59-60.

[191]Source: Beulah Collins, collector, *For Benefit of Clergy*, p. 55.

[192]Source: Cal and Rose Samra, *Holy Hilarity*, pp. 18-19.

[193]Source: J. Vernon Jacobs, compiler, *450 True Stories from Church History*, p. 100.

[194]Source: Hiley H. Ward, editor, *Ecumania*, p. 99.

[195]Source: Gary Holloway, *Saints, Demons, and Asses*, p. 19.

[196]Source: William Woughter, *All Preachers of Our God & King*, pp. 55-56.

[197]Source: Edward K. Rowell, editor, *Humor for Preaching and Teaching*, p. 142.

[198]Source: Cal and Rose Samra, *More Holy Hilarity*, p. 83.

[199]Source: Kurt Klinger, *A Pope Laughs*, p. 95.

[200]Source: Joey Adams, *The God Bit*, pp. 163-164.

[201]Source: Henri Fesquet, collector, *Wit and Wisdom of Good Pope John*, p. 42.

[202] Source: Bill Russell, *Red and Me: My Coach, My Lifelong Friend*, pp. 4-5.

[203]Source: Irvin C. Poley and Ruth Verlenden Poley, *Friendly Anecdotes*, pp. 113-114.

[204]Source: Alyene Porter, *Papa was a Preacher*, pp. 127-128.

[205]Source: Thomas Cleary, translator, *Zen Antics*, pp. 11-13.

[206]Source: Helen White Charles, collector and editor, *Quaker Chuckles*, p. 52.

[207]Source: Tom Mullen, *Living Longer and Other Sobering Possibilities*, . 112.

[208]Source: Don Wade, *"And Then Arnie Told Chi Chi...,"* p. 183.

[209]Source: Christina Lessa, *Women Who Win*, p. 63.

[210]Source: Joyce Goldenstern, *American Women Against Violence*, p. 25.

[211]Source: James W. Morrissey, *Noted Men and Women*, p. 15.

[212] Source: James Fadiman and Robert Frager, *Essential Sufism*, p. 187.

[213] Source: Laurie Lindop, *Athletes*, p. 30.

[214] Source: Massud Farzan, *Another Way of Laughter*, p. 45.

[215] Source: Karyn McLaughlin Frist, editor, *"Love you, Daddy Boy": Daughters Honor the Fathers They Love*, pp. 165-166.

[216] Source: Henri Fesquet, collector, *Wit and Wisdom of Good Pope John*, p. 78.

[217] Source: Lois Cantwell and Pohla Smith, *Women Winners: Then and Now*, pp. 17-18.

[218] Source: Patty Fox, *Star Style: Hollywood Legends as Fashion Icons*, p. 62.

[219] Source: Shmuel Himelstein, *Words of Wisdom, Words of Wit*, pp. 184-185.

[220] Source: Shmuel Himelstein, *A Touch of Wisdom, A Touch of Wit*, pp. 170-171.

[221] Source: Yitta Halberstam Mandelbaum, *Holy Brother*, pp. 83-84.

[222] Source: Philip Goodman, *Rejoice in Thy Festival*, pp. 24-25.

[223] Source: Jakob J. Petuchowski, translator and editor, *Our Masters Taught*, pp. 7-8.

[224] Source: Philip Goodman, *Rejoice in Thy Festival*, pp. 120-121.

[225] Source: Ross Phares, *Bible in Pocket, Gun in Hand*, pp. 142-143.

[226] Source: William B. Silverman, *Rabbinic Wisdom and Jewish Values*, p. 34.

[227] Source: Stan Banker, *Walk Cheerfully the Middleroad*, p. 145.

[228] Source: A. Monroe Aurand, Jr., *Wit and Humor of the Pennsylvania Germans*, p. 30.

[229] Source: R.R. Knudson, *Martina Navratilova: Tennis Power*, p. 35.

[230] Source: William R. Gerler, *Educator's Treasury of Humor for All Occasions*, p. 195.

[231] Source: Kerri Strug, *Landing on My Feet*, p. 148.

[232] Source: Christina Lessa, *Women Who Win*, p. 31.

[233] Source: Lynn Haney, *Perfect Balance*, p. 25.

[234] Source: Jeff Savage, *Julie Foudy: Soccer Superstar*, pp. 27-29.

[235] Source: Mary Malone, *Maya Lin: Architect and Artist*, p. 17-18, 23.

[236] Source: Rabbi Joseph Telushkin, *Jewish Wisdom*, pp. 230-231.

[237] Source: I.T. Frary, *At Large in Marble Halls*, pp. 84-85.

[238]Source: Irvin C. Poley and Ruth Verlenden Poley, *Friendly Anecdotes*, p. 118.

[239]Source: Harvey Mindess, *The Chosen People?*, p. 41.

[240]Source: Tom Mullen, *Seriously, Life is a Laughing Matter*, p. 13.

[241]Source: Louis Michaels, *The Humor and Warmth of Pope John XXIII*, p. 26.

[242]Source: Henri Fesquet, collector, *Wit and Wisdom of Good Pope John*, p. 69.

[243] Source: Tom Danehy, "Text your friends: Tom thinks something's wrong with youngsters today." *Tucson Weekly*. 6 August 2009 <http://www.tucsonweekly.com/tucson/danehy/Content?category=1063741>.

[244]Source: Malcolm Glenn Wyer, *Books and People*, p. 19-21.

[245]Source: Leah Furman, *Jennifer Lopez*, pp. 10-11.

[246]Source: Idries Shah, *The Pleasantries of the Incredible Mulla Nasrudin*, p. 67.

[247]Source: Jeff Savage, *Julie Krone: Unstoppable Jockey*, pp. 25-26.

[248]Source: Boze Hadleigh, *Hollywood Gays*, p. 367.

[249]Source: Chih Chung Tsai, *Zen Speaks*, p. 26.

[250]Source: Perle Besserman and Manfred Steger, *Crazy Clouds*, p. 39.

www.ingramcontent.com/pod-product-compliance
Lightning Source LLC
Chambersburg PA
CBHW021124130726
47988CB00003B/1151